Problem-solving Processes
of College Students

SUPPLEMENTARY EDUCATIONAL MONOGRAPHS
Published in conjunction with THE SCHOOL REVIEW
and THE ELEMENTARY SCHOOL JOURNAL

Number 73 · July 1950

Problem-solving Processes of College Students

An Exploratory Investigation

BY

BENJAMIN S. BLOOM

College Examiner and Associate Professor of Education
University of Chicago

LOIS J. BRODER

Research Assistant, University Examiner's Office
University of Chicago

THE UNIVERSITY OF CHICAGO PRESS
CHICAGO 37 · ILLINOIS

THE UNIVERSITY OF CHICAGO PRESS, CHICAGO 37
Cambridge University Press, London, N.W. 1, England
W. J. Gage & Co., Limited, Toronto 2B, Canada

TABLE OF CONTENTS

CHAPTER 1

THE ANALYSIS OF MENTAL PROCESSES
RATHER THAN MENTAL PRODUCTS

Possible values in analyzing mental processes rather than mental products

Mental processes represent a very difficult and complex subject for study. To a large extent, we have been limited in this study by the widespread emphasis on overt behavior as the major acceptable type of evidence on the workings of the mind. Much of psychological research attempts to infer from the observed behavior of the individual what the mental processes must have been. This attempt to make an objective science of psychology not only limits the kinds of data acceptable to the psychologist but must necessarily make for many inaccuracies in his inferences about the nature of the mental processes.

The handicap placed on the work of the psychologist by the type of data he regards as useful and scientific is well demonstrated in the field of individual differences. Much of the work in this field is based on the use of various types of tests. In these tests the subject is presented with questions which he is to answer and problems which he is to solve. After some mental effort, the subject submits his answers or solutions for appraisal by the tester. In addition, the tester may secure observations of the behavior of the subject while taking the test. From these data the tester will attempt to draw conclusions about the mental characteristics of the subject. What is missing is information on the process by which the problems are solved. The meth-

Figure Analogies

In each line below, find the rule by which Figure A is changed to make Figure B. Apply the rule to Figure C. Select the resulting figure at the right and blacken the corresponding answer space.

Figure 1*

ods of attack, the steps in the thinking process, the kinds of considerations used to make one choice rather than another, and the feelings and attitudes of the subject are neglected or given very little attention. The products of thought – the answers to the questions or the solutions to the problems – plus the observations may give the tester a fleeting glimpse into the complex

*L. L. Thurstone and Thelma Gwinn Thurstone, American Council on Education Psychological Examination for College Freshmen, 1943 edition. Princeton, New Jersey: Cooperative Test Division, Educational Testing Service.

processes of thought involved, but usually this is incomplete and, almost of necessity, inaccurate.

If it were established that the evidence on overt behavior or the products of thought had a clear-cut and definite relationship to the mental processes which produced them, the psychologist would appear to have ample justification for limiting his data to such objective and easily observed phenomena. However, even the most simple exploratory studies on responses to test questions reveal that the same solution or product of thought may be arrived at by distinctly different processes of thought. For example, students were given the problem shown in Figure 1. When asked to "think aloud" as they attacked this problem, the following reports were obtained from students:

John J: "One-half circle, so one-half square — Number 4."

Edward F: "Figure A is halved to make B, so Figure C is halved to make Number 4."

Dorothy S: "A to B — merely cut A. C to 1 — turn C to equal 1. I think that's the nearest — no, to cut C equals 4."

Betty K: "Oh, they're taking away half of it, so the answer would be 4."

Thomas N: "I have an idea of something which is the left half of a whole -- seeing this is a square, be looking for the left half of a square and find 4 right away."

George R: "Geometrical, I guess. Circle and one-half of a circle cut off to the left. Square and one-half of a square cut off to the left. I choose 4."

All six students got the correct answer. Thus, the solution or final product of the thought would all be the same for the tester. However, these brief reports from psychologically naïve subjects reveal that the process of thought involved (insofar as it is revealed by this method of reporting) differs from one subject to another. Several of the students thought in terms of the operation of cutting or halving the figure, while the others evidently thought in terms of an operation which had already been completed; that is, they had been presented with wholes and halves. Some of the students thought (or expressed their thoughts) in terms of circles and squares, while others thought in terms of abstract figures which could be referred to by such symbols as A, B, C, and 4. Their rules differed considerably in generality. Some apply only to the specific illustrations given, while others apply to any combination of figures whether they be squares, circles, triangles, rectangles, etc.

Only two students appeared to think in terms of the left half of the figures. In this particular example, this level of precision was unnecessary, since only the left half of the square was given as a possible answer. However, one wonders what answer would have been selected by the different students if they were given as possible answers the left half of a square, the right half of the square, and the bottom or top half. Dorothy S. was apparently led astray by something and proceeded to select an incorrect answer, which she very quickly changed to the correct response. The final product does not reflect this temporary difficulty. In these reports, we are able to detect differences in the completeness of the record of the process of thought, differences in the method of attacking or thinking about the prob-lem, and differences in the level of generality at which the problem was solved. None of these differences is revealed by the record of the answer or the choice selected.

The psychologist studying individual differences through the use of tests and questionnaires of various kinds must, if he is to interpret the results with any degree of accuracy, investigate the nature of the mental processes underlying the responses to these instruments. He will undoubtedly find more variation in the thought-processes leading to the responses than there is in the responses themselves. An investigation of thought-processes would probably mean that the psychologist must study relatively small numbers of subjects under adequately controlled conditions rather than make the large-scale type of study ordinarily employed in investigations of individual differences. The former type of investigation would require not only large amounts of data on these subjects but also the development of new techniques for studying thought-processes.

One possible outcome of this type of research could be the development of tests and questionnaires which would more adequately reflect the varia-tions in thought-processes. At present, aptitude and achievement tests are analyzed to show the speed and accuracy of the subject's solutions to the problems presented, while little or no attention is given to the methods by which the solutions were obtained. It should be possible to construct test sit-uations such that each of a variety of methods of attack would be reflected in a different solution. If such test situations could be constructed, it would then be possible to infer the nature of the thought-processes from the nature of the answers or solutions recalled or selected – that is, from the products of thought.

The educator, as well as the psychologist, assumes a correspondence between mental products and processes. He usually assumes that the indi-vidual who has the largest number of correct responses on the final examina-tion is the individual with the best or most desirable quality of mental proc-esses. Even in classroom discussions, the teacher is generally more con-cerned about the accuracy of responses than about the methods by which the student arrived at his responses or solutions. In large part, this preoccupa-tion with accuracy of responses is a consequence of the difficulties of getting information about the processes of thought, the limitations of time, the large size of classes, and the pressure for coverage of subject matter. In spite of this emphasis on the products of thought, educators usually agree that good habits (or processes) of thought are the important and significant outcomes of education. Also, they would probably agree that the particular solutions or answers given to schoolroom problems are of little consequence except insofar as they serve to indicate the quality of the student's thinking.

Until the educator knows and understands the relations between the so-lutions given by the students to academic problems and the thought-processes which led to the solutions, he is unable to determine whether instructional procedures are effective. If the educator is attempting to inculcate good hab-its of thinking, he must be able to determine when and under what conditions such good habits are established. Present emphasis on accuracy of solutions undoubtedly gives a misleading picture about the nature of the student's thinking.

The educator also has a serious problem in accounting for academic failure. Educational institutions tolerate a very high proportion of failure and ascribe much of it to variations in intelligence or aptitude, motivation, and effort. A study of the nature of thought-processes should reveal the extent to which the student's habits of thinking are an important factor responsible for academic success or failure. It should reveal where and under what conditions educational procedures lead to good and poor habits of thinking. It should also reveal something about the ways in which the student's habits of thinking can be improved and the extent to which remediation of poor habits of thinking leads to increased success or accuracy in solving academic problems.

The educator and the psychologist are faced with three alternatives:

1. They can, as they are now doing, give their primary attention to the products of thought and almost completely ignore the processes of thought. This, in the writers' opinion, must inevitably mean educational procedures and psychological research which are inappropriate, superficial, and, in all likelihood, incorrect.

2. They can perform experiments which may enable them to establish a high relationship between the products and the processes of thought. If such a relationship can be established, they will need to be concerned only with the more readily observed products and can infer the processes from these observations. Such a relationship is, in the writers' opinion, not likely to be established. However, it should be possible to set up methods of observing the products of thought which will enable the educator and the psychologist to make somewhat more accurate inferences about the processes of thought.

3. They can develop techniques which will make possible the securing of evidence on both the processes and the products of thought. Much difficulty can be anticipated in securing evidence about the processes, and perhaps the nature of the human organism is such as to prevent the securing of any clear-cut and objective evidence on these processes. In any case, attention on the processes of thought must mean the development of new techniques for psychological research. It may also require a change from large-scale testing and mass studies to those which involve small numbers of subjects studied by rather intensive techniques. The question of whether such research would be fruitful, or even possible, can be answered only after many serious attempts have been made. The challenging nature of the problem and the tremendous possibilities which would arise from a successful attack and solution should serve to channel much of our research effort to this field.

It should be noted that concern about processes of thought is evident in the work of some educators and psychologists. In schools where tutorial methods and small-class discussion methods are utilized, the instructor is frequently as much concerned about the student's methods of thinking as about the results of his thinking. The clinical psychologist is especially concerned with probing into the individual's intellectual and emotional characteristics. He is frequently concerned about the ways in which an individual thinks about certain problems as well as the basis for these thoughts. Some of the methods experimental psychologists have used to study mental processes are discussed in the next section of this chapter.

Methods of analyzing mental processes reported in the literature

A survey of the literature concerning methods analyzing mental processes indicates the use of two major avenues of approach. The first method of analysis is that of inferring the mental process from the observed product of thought — for example, taking a subject's final solution to a particular problem and, from that, inferring how he must have proceeded toward this solution. The second method is that of exploring the process itself — that is, investigating the subject's thoughts, feelings, and reactions as he attacks the problem.

Inferring the process from the product. — Much experimentation involving inferences about the process of problem-solving from the product has been done in the field of comparative psychology. Lloyd Morgan's descriptions of trial-and-error behavior in animals (14), Thorndike's experiments with the classical puzzle-box problems (19), and Köhler's studies on insight in anthropoids (8) illustrate this work. The general procedure in animal experimentation is for the experimenter to set up clearly defined problems and to infer the thought-processes from the animal's actions. Many experimenters in this field are reluctant to explain the animal's actions in terms of thinking processes and report only that the animal exhibited behavior X rather than behavior Y or Z. Occasionally an animal experimenter attempts to analogize the animal's behavior to that of humans. No matter how completely and carefully such experiments are conducted, it is clearly impossible to determine the thought-processes of the animal as it attacked a problem or reached a solution. The primary limitation on all animal experimentation is the obvious fact that the animals lack speech, and the experimenter's inferences about the mental processes can never be corroborated.

Many very careful and well-controlled experiments have been conducted with children and adults in a further attempt to define the process of problem-solving from a study of the product. The general approach to this type of study is illustrated by Heidbreder (5) and Maier (13). These experiments usually employ puzzle-type problems, where the results of problem-solving in terms of success or failure are relatively clear cut. The experimenter observes the overt behavior of the subject as well as the solution given. From this, he attempts to infer what the process of problem-solving might have been. Studies involving differential age groups, hierarchies of problem complexity, and other differential factors have been made.

Attempts to infer the mental processes from observations of overt behavior and data on the final product or solution are subject to error. It would appear possible for a variety of mental processes to lead to the same end product or solution. Unless the experimenter secures further and more direct evidence on the processes involved, he cannot be certain about his inferences of process from product.

A somewhat different approach to the investigation of the nature of the mental processes from a study of the products is that of Piaget (17). Piaget tried to determine the nature of, and the steps in, the process of childish reasoning by examining the language of the children, their spontaneous talk, and their answers to specific questions. He used this method in studying different age groups.

Actual exploration of mental processes. — The second major method of determining the processes of thought, that of analysis of the processes themselves, involves retrospection and introspection.

Retrospection consists in securing narrative accounts from individuals or groups after they have completed a process or experience. Some of this work in problem-solving has been done with the experimenter serving as both experimenter and subject. Thus, Dewey (4) reports the ways in which he attacked certain problems and the considerations which led to one solution as opposed to another. Another example of the retrospective technique is to be found in Wertheimer's Productive Thinking (21). He reports on a number of problems, including the thinking that led Einstein to the theory of relativity.

There are several objections to the use of retrospection in studying the nature of mental processes. It is very difficult for a person to remember all the steps in his thought-processes and to report them in the way in which they originally occurred. There is a tendency on the part of the narrator to edit the report, to set forth the process in a nicely logical order. Things seem to tie together so concisely after the problem has been solved. The narrator will usually omit errors and "dead ends" in his thinking processes. He will not remember the queer quirks and unusual circumstances which surrounded his thinking. Such reports generally present a coherent and well-ordered train of thought rather than the incoherent and jumbled process which may have occurred. The editing is done unconsciously to a large extent, but it tends to introduce a bias into the data obtained. These retrospective accounts are useful, but it must be recognized that they are rebuilt outlines of thought-processes and tend to reveal only the high spots and finished products rather than the raw materials and details in a fantastically complex series of thought steps.

Introspective studies, such as Titchener's, attempt to analyze mental processes by obtaining detailed reports from the subjects about their thoughts, reactions, and feelings as they perform certain tasks (20). Such studies require highly trained subjects and are exhaustively time-consuming. They can, however, provide a very complete picture of the complexities of the thought-processes.

Other possible methods

Several other possible methods of analyzing mental processes in problem-solving should be considered. The test worker may develop test questions in which a single type of problem is presented in different ways. He may then determine the frequency of each correct solution and each type of error under the different conditions for the problem. With these data before him, the test worker can try to determine why the problem was difficult for the subjects or how the subjects happened to give each of the answers. He can never be quite sure, however, that he is not going beyond the implications of his data. He cannot accurately determine why one answer was chosen in preference to another, where the student might have gone off in his reasoning, nor the ways in which the subject may have misinterpreted the question. Under these circumstances, the inferences about the processes from the products are uncertain and are unlikely to reveal fully the nature of the thought-processes.

Another possible avenue for investigation of the processes of thought is that of inferring these processes from the rules of formal logic — that is, that one step in reasoning must follow another in logical sequence. This approach tends to describe the ideal attack, where the final goal is reached with a minimum of effort and a step-like precision. It is quite unlikely that, for the majority of people, the process of reasoning actually takes place in this economical and orderly fashion.

As has already been indicated, if it were possible to design a problem such that each solution must be arrived at by a unique method of attack, the objections to inferring process from product would be overcome. It would then be unnecessary to ask the subject to tell how he attacked the problem, since his solution would contain within it all the evidence needed on the method employed. As yet, the writers have seen no very good example of a problem which meets such criteria. Perhaps it will be possible to devise ingenious problems in which there is a one-to-one relationship between the process and the product. Such problems would make research on thought-processes clear, objective, and economical.

Some exploratory efforts in analyzing the nature of mental processes

A possible point of departure in analyzing the nature of mental processes in relation to the products of thought is through investigations of problem-solving. Problems can be selected for which only a limited number of solutions are appropriate, although the methods by which the solutions are reached cannot be so easily limited. It is possible to select problems such that some can be solved quickly and simply by the subject, while others tax the subjects's mental resources to the utmost. It would also seem possible to find problems which require the subject to make use of relatively clear and easily reported mental processes.

For this type of investigation, problem-solving may be regarded as the process by which the subject goes from the problem or task as he sees it to the solution which he regards as meeting the demands of the problem. A problem may be regarded as a task which the subject is able to understand but for which he does not have an immediate solution. It is expected that, although the subject will be somewhat perplexed, he will not be utterly confused.

In an effort to understand more about the nature of problems and the processes of thinking involved in problem-solving, an investigation was started at the University of Chicago in the spring of 1945. Since we were primarily interested in the problems that students must solve in an academic environment, the problems were selected from the various tests and examinations which are given to students in the College of the University of Chicago.

For the purposes of this investigation, we rejected examination questions in which memory for specific information appeared to be the sole factor in securing a solution. We were not interested in studying the ways in which an individual recalls specific information, nor did we believe such questions would reveal much about the nature of the mental processes. For example, it does not appear to be much of a problem if the student is asked, "Who wrote Paradise Lost?" since this can only be answered if the student has associated Milton with the book and if he now remembers this association. If the student has the correct answer, he is usually able to give it quickly but is unable to report much about how he got the solution other than to tell the investigator that he "remembered the answer."

We also rejected, for purposes of this study, problems which appeared

7

to be merely puzzles and which required little more than the proper manual or mental manipulations. By puzzles we are referring to problems which can be solved only through trial and error because it is impossible to see in advance the consequences of particular actions and manipulations.

We attempted to select problems for which the subject would have clear-cut, although perhaps quite complex, goals to achieve and for which he could make a conscious plan of attack. In many cases, these problems involved knowledge of specific information, although such information was not the sole requisite for a correct solution. We limited the problems to questions and test situations taken from various academic tests and examinations. This was done because students in school are expected to solve such problems, and most of the students accept them as problems to be solved. Although it is expected that problem-solving is just as real and far more earnest when the student encounters "real-life" problems, the very nature of these problems makes it difficult to analyze them. In "real-life" problems, the values and goals of individuals play a large part in the attack and many solutions are equally appropriate and correct, depending upon the point of view from which the individual has started. The examination problems, on the other hand, involve rather clear-cut solutions and, to a large extent, are so oriented as to divorce values from the problem-solving situation. The examination problems are very clearly structured, and competent individuals in a subject field can agree on the solution regarded as most correct or adequate.

It was, of course, recognized that the same question or test situation might not represent the same problem for every subject who faces it. The students may differ in the extent to which they possess the relevant information required in the solution of the problem, the extent to which they have previously encountered similar problems, and the extent to which they are willing to make an effort to solve a particular problem. The way in which each student looks at a particular task may make it a unique problem for him. It is, of course, the task of investigations like this to determine the ways in which problems are interpreted and the nature of the thinking which leads to a given solution.

In order to secure data on the thoughts, feelings, and methods used by students when attacking this group of problems, an attempt was made to get each student to "think aloud" as he worked the problems. This technique had been used by Buswell and John (3) to diagnose difficulties in arithmetic. The students were given a brief training period on the technique of thinking aloud as they attacked simple arithmetical problems. When the student was asked to multiply 5 x 6, he gave the answer at once and was unable to report the steps by which he solved the problem. However, when presented with a more complex problem, 34 x 89, the student was able to tell what he was doing as he multiplied the numbers and added the products of 4 x 89 and 30 x 89. After a series of problems like this, the student was given several simple verbal problems. When the interviewer judged that the student was giving a relatively adequate picture of his mental processes as he attacked each problem, the student was given the selected problems for which data were to be secured.

As the student thought aloud on each of the problems, the interviewer took as complete notes as possible on everything the student said and did. From time to time, it was found necessary to supplement these notes by asking the student to recall what he had done after he had completed a problem. This was necessary when the student spoke too rapidly for the interviewer to take notes and when the student's report on his thoughts did not yield a complete picture of the problem-solving process. Best results were obtained when the student reported his thoughts by mumbling. If he spoke loudly and clearly, it was noticed that he seemed to be doing many of the operations twice — once for himself and once for the interviewer.

Examples of problem-solving

A few of the problems included in this study are presented below. These problems are accompanied by the solutions and the reports on the methods by which they were attacked. The reports were almost verbatim recordings and, in many cases, appear to be rambling and confused. In many cases, the reports are incomplete and do not reveal all the considerations the subject must have had in mind in order to reach his solution. Frequently the subject expresses his thinking in incomplete sentences, and occasionally the grammatical form is quite incorrect. An English purist might be horrified to note the extent to which the students think, or at least express their thoughts, in a grammatical form quite different from that used by the same subjects in speaking or writing.

The three problems to be presented were selected because they illustrate some of the characteristics revealed by the techniques of problem-solving analysis discussed in this monograph. Although the problems represent only a limited sample of the types of problems which students encounter, relatively clear-cut differences are apparent from problem to problem as well as from student to student for each problem. The contrast between the student's score (or number of correct answers) for each problem and the reports on what he did and said when attacking the problem reveals some of the values of this type of research.

In most cases, the reports or protocols are arranged in order of score on the problem as well as in order of clarity and effectiveness of problem-solving. Thus, some of the first protocols are vague, wandering, and, to a large extent, not productive of correct solutions. These first reports also reveal little about the process of problem-solving. The later reports in a series are usually more clear, direct, and productive.

The reader will find this material of greatest value and interest if he attempts to solve each of the problems before reading the protocols for that problem.

Responses on Problem 1. — The responses of six students to the first problem (Figure 2) are presented below.

Pauline M. (Score 0): (Read the directions — laughed.) "Something I don't know anything about — guess on all problems — seems plants would be first — don't know what the sponges are since I don't know sponges — would probably get them all mixed up — might say sponges second, only guessing — say amphibians — last, I believe, mammals and fishes — all guesswork, though."

This student looked at the problem and apparently decided that this was a totally unfamiliar field and that her plan of attack would be one of guessing. Her placement of the plants first would seem to indicate some basis other than guesswork for the ranking, although she was apparently unaware or un-

9

able to report it. It is probable that she divided life forms into plants and animals and regarded plants as coming first. Her claim of lack of knowledge about sponges may have represented a defense in case the solution was incorrect. She ranked the remaining items in some order without revealing a basis for the order, although she again repeated that it was all guesswork. Throughout the attack there was evidence of very little confidence in her ability to get the correct answers and little evidence of an attempt to reason through to a solution.

Problem 1

Rank the following life forms in the order of their appearance in the geologic record. Blacken the answer space A for the one that appeared first, etc.
> 81. Mammals
> 82. Sponges
> 83. Amphibians
> 84. Fishes
> 85. Flowering plants

Figure 2

Mary W. (Score 1): (Read the directions.) "Not quite sure I read the right thing, so re-read the directions — don't understand if I'm to pick one of each of these for A or if A for the first and B for the second, and so on — haven't had Biological Sciences, so I'll just venture a guess — undoubtedly wrong — not mammals, or fishes — don't know amphibians — if that's what it is — say eeny, meeny, miny, mo — and sponges — 82 for A — assume if in front A, B, C, D, E rate them in order — don't know exactly what to do with the ones left over."

As she read the directions, she did not appear to be able to grasp the nature of the problem and had difficulty in relating the first sentence of the directions to the second. The student's reference to not having taken a biological sciences course, her statement that the answers are to be based on a guess which will undoubtedly be wrong, and her elaborate effort at selection of an answer by chance methods — all indicate her lack of confidence in her knowledge and ability to solve the problem. It is interesting to note that she is willing to try the problem even though she is so unsure of herself. The limitations of this report make it difficult to determine on what basis mammals or fish were rejected and why her chance selection scheme was restricted to the two or three out of the five possible choices. After selecting a choice for A, she again indicated confusion about directions but had apparently given up the idea of placing the life forms in order. Her final remark would indicate that she was not fully satisfied that the problem had been completed.

Val H. (Score 0): (Read the directions.) "A appeared first, B next, D — the period most recently — first 85 — recall from biology, answer A — then 82 would be B — then not sure of amphibians or fishes — there were primitive fishes, but — say fishes third, then amphibians D, and then 81 E for I

10

think they are most recent."

The limited "thinking aloud" makes it difficult to determine exactly on what basis this student attacked the problem. There is some indication, however, that he differentiated fish into primitive and other types. There is evidence ("recall from biology") that he determined the answers on the basis of specific information remembered. The restatement of the directions seemed to be of help to this student in deciding what must be done. It is of interest to note that, in restating the directions, he did not make provision for a fifth form, or E. However, the mechanics of the problem apparently corrected this. The emphasis on type of fish – primitive versus other – seemed to be of some help in determining the position of amphibians. It should be noted that this student did not make the elaborate protests of inadequacy which characterized the preceding reports. Although this student had the correct order for all except flowering plants, the method of scoring used would give him the same zero score as Pauline, who clearly did not understand the problem and who did not know how to attack it.

David F. (Score 1): "Rank — (Read the directions.) Does that mean phylogenetic tree – I know the phylogenetic tree better than the geologic record – mammals late in the animal kingdom – flowering plants late in the plant kingdom – sponges is the answer – check – mammals after sponges, sponges before amphibians, amphibians before fishes, fishes before flowering plants, sponges before all of them, so sponges first."

In spite of his emphasis on the word "rank," it is not clear whether David ever clearly understood the nature of the problem or whether he forgot what he was to do. This student translated the problem from one of ranking the items in order of appearance in the geologic record to one of ranking them in order of their position on the phylogenetic tree. This equating of the phylogenetic tree and the geologic record appears to be a legitimate method and is apparently an effective method of changing a problem into a more workable form. It is not clear whether the student remembered the positions of the various life forms on the phylogenetic tree or whether he was considering the characteristics of each as the method of placing it on the tree. The distinction between animal and plant kingdom and position within each kingdom appeared to be a helpful organization and guide to further thinking about the problem. After considering three of the five life forms, the student selected an answer and then went through a fairly elaborate checking process in which he compared pairs of items.

Ned M. (Score 2): (Read the statement. Read the alternatives, mispronouncing "amphibians.") "Mammals last and fishes next – no, mammals last – no, my biology course in the ninth grade – mammals, no flowering plants last because had cavemen and animals when only had ferns – third, phyla, and flowering plants in the fourth – then mammals, fishes, going backwards – flowering plants, mammals, fishes, don't know what amphibians are, but sponges are third from the bottom of lowest animal life, so amphibians last along with amoeba – amphi, amphi, can't remember."

This student was apparently unfamiliar with the term "amphibian," and it became a source of difficulty. It is interesting to observe that he started from the most recent and attempted to work back, which is the reverse of the method by which the answers are to be recorded. The system of placing flowering plants last appeared to involve a kind of proof based on his evidence that mammals existed when primitive forms of plants also existed. This student seemed to have a mental picture of phyla, since he talked about third and fourth phyla and also spoke of lowest animal life in terms of "bottom." He seems to have attempted to place the one unknown item (amphibian) by establishing a relationship with a known form which sounds similar (the amoeba). In general, then, this student seemed to have a mental picture of phyla in mind, and his task was that of relating the specific forms given to their possible position in the order of phyla. (After the problem had been completed, the student was asked whether he knew what an amphibious tank was. He replied immediately and quickly grasped the correct order of the amphibians in this problem.)

Bernice Y. (Score 3): (Read the directions. Read the alternatives.) "Fish before the land animals, therefore fishes first – no, sponges first, sponges on the cellular level of development – well, minimum of differentiation – then fishes, differentiated structures, gills – amphibians, the bridge – life from water to earth – flowering plants next, no, flowering plants are plants, rest are animals – either flowering plants or mammals last, no, not true – flowering plants late on the evolutionary scale – flowering plants 4, and mammals 5; very latest, highest degree of development."

Here the subject appeared to be using two bases for decisions and using them interchangeably. One was that water life forms preceded land life forms while another basis was that life forms should be in the order of level of development. She began with the distinction between water and land forms but, as this basis proved inadequate, she made use of the level of development and differentiation. In each case, she had a principle in mind, as well as the characteristics of each of the life forms which enabled her to make use of the principle. Her method of resolving the position of mammals and flowering plants was not clearly indicated. In general, however, this represents a fairly complete picture of her method of attach on the problem. It reveals an attack of a very high order; the student had a systematic method which she was able to keep in mind throughout the problem-solving process.

Comments on Problem 1 and the reports. – In solving this problem, the student must first realize that it is one in which he is to rank items in a particular order. The fact that the directions are somewhat abbreviated may have proved a stumbling block for some of the students. However, a careful student should have little difficulty in understanding the problem from the directions given here. After the student has the problem in mind, he may use different bases for his ranking. Thus, he may place them in order on the basis of memory of the geologic record or the evolutionary tree. He may also make use of such bases as differentiation between water and land forms, between plant and animal kingdom, and between more complex and less complex life forms. In addition to having a particular principle or basis for ranking, the student must know a sufficient amount about each of the life forms to select the characteristics which enable him to apply the principle in each case. This involves the isolation of the particular characteristics of the life form which are most relevant to the principles he is using.

If the accuracy of the answers – the products of thinking – were the only criterion, the individual students would be placed into four groups:

> Score of 0 ..... Pauline and Val
> Score of 1 ..... Mary and David
> Score of 2 ..... Ned
> Score of 3 ..... Bernice

There is little question that Ned and Bernice understood the problem best and employed superior techniques of solving this problem when compared with the other students. However, the scores do not adequately reflect the variations among these students. Thus, Val apparently knew the order of all except flowering plants but received no credit, since his error in the placement of plants made all the others wrong. But even more important than the scoring and the errors it produces is the lack of evidence on such factors indicated in the notes as:

1. The presence of systematic methods of analyzing and attacking the problem (best exemplified by Bernice's attempt).

2. The technique by which a problem is converted to a more meaningful form (best exemplified by David).

3. The extent to which a single error throws off the entire solution to a problem (best exemplified by Val).

4. The effect of failure to understand the nature of the task or the requirements of a problem (best exemplified by Mary).

5. The effect of forgetting the requirements of the problem (this is probably what happened to David).

6. The extent to which the individual makes an effort (at least in the problem-solving interview situations) to indicate his lack of knowledge, the necessity of using chance methods, and his expectancy of failure (exemplified by Mary and Pauline). The elaborate set of comments on lack of confidence in ability to solve the problem may indicate a real inadequacy. It is quite possible, however, that the student does this to protect his feelings against a probable failure. However, we have noted similar comments by students who were successful in solving a problem as well as those who were not.

Responses on Problem 2. – The problem-solving techniques employed by six students in another problem (Figure 3) are analyzed below.

Roy C. (Score 0): (Read the directions.) "Don't do that (blacken answer space). (Read the statements. Read the alternatives.) Say D – Usually when men strike they have a reason for it – if they don't, then their jobs are at stake."

Although this is not a very complete report on the student's problem-solving, it is clear that he lost sight of the true nature of the problem and selected a conclusion for reasons other than those of logical relation to the original statements. The conclusion he selected apparently involved a personal judgment about the desirability of strikes. This lack of objectivity when faced with a problem set in a context involving value considerations is a frequent source of error for many students.

Problem 2

DIRECTIONS: In each of the following items, you are given statements and four conclusions. Assume that the statements are true. You are to judge which of the conclusions then logically follows; i.e., must be true if the statements are true. Blacken the answer space corresponding to the one conclusion which logically follows. If none of the conclusions logically follows, blacken answer space E.

STATEMENTS:

Any action that impedes the war effort of the United States should be made illegal.

All strikes impede the war effort of the United States.

CONCLUSIONS:

A – All strikes should be made illegal.
B – Some restrictions should be placed on the right to strike, but it would be unwise to make them all illegal.
C – Some strikes should be made illegal.
D – Unjustifiable strikes should be made illegal.
E – None of the foregoing conclusions follows.

Figure 3

Louis S. (Score 0): (Read the directions emphasizing "Assume the statements are true." Read the statements and each of the alternatives.) "Say B, that would be not only logic, but also using my interpretation of equity."

In spite of the fact this student emphasized the part of the directions which makes clear that the statements must be accepted as true for this problem, he was unable to keep it in mind throughout the problem. There is little evidence as to the considerations which led him to select answer B, but it is interesting to note that he regarded it both as meeting the requirements of the problem and as satisfying his own ideas about what is equitable. Louis was apparently somewhat more clearly aware of the nature of the problem than was Roy, even though both selected the wrong answer. One senses a note of satisfaction in Louis' solution – it is (for him) both logically correct and ethically right.

14

John D. (Score 1): (Read the directions and the statements. Read the list of conclusions.) "According to these statements, say A because strikes impede the war effort, so should be made illegal — not my comment, but according to what the statements say."

This student recognized his own attitude on the subject, but he was fully aware of the basis on which he was to select a conclusion to satisfy the requirements of the problem. He appears to have substituted the word "strike" from the minor premise for the phrase "any action" in the major premise — probably as a test of the correctness of the conclusion. Although he gave some consideration to the other conclusions, this record does not reveal the nature of his thinking about them.

Martin S. (Score 1): (Read the directions. Read the statements.) "Have to do this again. (Re-read the directions.) Four conclusions — five conclusions — two statements here that are true — two statements. (Re-read the statements. Read all the conclusions.) Any action. (Read the statements.) Then, A should follow if all strikes impede war effort of the United States — remember Mr. P's, and X's and Y's."

This student had difficulty in determining exactly what material he was working with and found it necessary to read the directions and statements several times. It is not clear on what basis he finally selected the answer, although his reference to P's, X's, and Y's may indicate use of letters as substitutes for the major terms or an attempt to remember a syllogism with a similar form.

Oliver K. (Score 1): (Read the directions slowly, pausing to understand as he goes along. Read the statement and each of the alternatives.) "A is the answer — the second proposition equals the third proposition — realized the answer at first, but still read through all."

This student seems to have performed some process of equating the propositions, although it is not clear exactly what was done. In spite of the fact that he read all the alternatives before reporting an answer, this student was of the opinion that he knew the correct answer before he read the alternatives. He was evidently not certain about the correctness of his solution and apparently felt some compulsion to read through the alternatives.

Allen G. (Score 1): (Read the directions and the statements.) "Then say, if a strike impedes the war effort of the U.S., then strike should be made illegal because it is an action — studying now in mathematics — knew the answer before looking."

This student also recognized the relationship between "strike" and "action." He, unlike the previous students, managed to determine the correct conclusion before even examining the alternatives given. This would indicate a relatively high degree of confidence in his ability to solve the problem.

Comments on **Problem 2** and the reports. — This problem is relatively simple and does not yield much information about the students' mental processes. We have found that, whenever a problem involves only a straightforward and mechanical manipulation of symbols, the student is unable to report much about this thinking. Thus, if a college student is asked to multiply 6 times 5 he will usually give an answer very quickly and will claim that the process was automatic and that he was not conscious of what he did. It is possible that a group of well-trained subjects could give a more complete introspective report, although for our purposes such a detailed report does not appear to be essential.

This problem requires the student to work with the terms of a fairly simple syllogism. Some complexity is added to the problem by its emotional or value context. The problem and the methods of solution here reported are of value in revealing:

1. The extent to which the individual has difficulty in keeping the requirements of a problem in mind when they are in conflict with his attitudes or values.

2. Some of the techniques by which students manipulate the terms in a simple syllogism. In this problem some students used a method of substituting one term for another; others used a method of equating certain of the terms and propositions; and another student either attempted to remember a similar syllogistic form or substituted letters for the terms in the syllogism.

3. The extent to which students differ in confidence about their problem-solving. Some students apparently find it unnecessary to read the alternatives offered and are able to determine a correct answer before referring to the alternatives. This appears to be a very different type of problem-solving than one where the student examines each of the alternative answers and then makes a choice.

Responses on Problem 3. – The thought-processes of six students solving Problem 3 (Figure 4) are analyzed below.

John N. (Score 0): (Read the introductory statements and read the directions incompletely.)
(Read item 26.) "No.
(Read item 27.) "Think about that.
(Read item 28.) "No — must be number 27, by the process of elimination."

This student, who evidently did not understand the nature of the problem, made it one of selecting the best of three statements rather than one of judging the relation of each statement to the policy of controlling the boom. In this report there is practically no evidence on the process of problem-solving It is of little value in determining why the student misunderstood the problem or on what basis he made his decision about item 27.

Stephen N. (Score 1): (Read the statements and the directions.)
(Read item 26.) "Forgot that reserve ratio – if you lower the reserve ratio would tend to control inflation – consistent, I think – would let less deposits out of the bank.
(Read item 27.) "Inconsistent — people would have more money for other things – would be runaway inflation.
(Read item 28.) "Forgot open market – if you buy in the open market –

know three ways for banks to have more reserve on hand – reserve ratio, something else, and open market – would be consistent, I think – can't remember how it operates – have to study economics some more."

This student attempted to remember relevant material he had studied at one time and made little effort to solve the problem on the basis of the given material. It is interesting to note that he translated the reserve into

---

Problem 3

Some economists feel that there is danger of an extreme inflationary boom after the war. It is the opinion of such economists that the government should control the boom in order to prevent a depression such as the one following the stockmarket crash of 1929.

Below are a number of specific suggestions. For each of the following items, blacken

answer space 1 – if it would be consistent with the policy
of controlling the boom;
answer space 2 – if it is directly inconsistent with the policy.

26. Lower the reserve that banks are required to hold against deposits

27. Reduce taxes considerably

28. Encourage the federal reserve banks to buy securities in the open market

---

Figure 4

a reserve ratio. He did not, however, grasp the correct relation between changes in reserves and release of deposits from the bank. In Item 27 the student correctly related reduction in taxes to amount of money available and to inflation. In Item 28 the student attempted to remember particular subject matter rather than think through the consequences of the item. He had great difficulty in solving other problems presented to him; to a large extent, this difficulty can be accounted for by his lack of independent thinking. In attempting to solve most problems, he tried to remember specific answers from textbooks, lectures, and discussions rather than make an effort to think through each problem on the basis of the given material. This student was not at all confident about his problem-solving and apparently found it necessary to make several excuses about his lack of memory for certain specifics.

Mary W. (Score 2): (Read the statements and the directions.)
(Read item 26.) "Look down to see what I'm supposed to do.

17

(Re-read the statements and the directions.) "Not quite sure what I'm doing so re-read for the third time. (Re-read the statements and the directions.)

(Re-read item 26.) "Not sure of this, so on to second one.

(Read item 27.) "Say inconsistent, because if there is inflationary boom, if people make more money, taxes have to keep up with it to take away the money so they can't spend it.

(Read item 28.) "Try to figure out what bearing that had exactly.

(Re-read item 26.) "I'm a time waster, say 26 would be consistent – no, that I know, banks have reserve – idea is to get people to deposit as much as possible – not answer 28.

(Re-read item 28.) "Say inconsistent, I feel it is."

This student had very little in the way of a systematic approach. She spent a good deal of time and effort jumping from one part of the problem to another and re-reading directions. She skipped the first item because she was uncertain of what was involved and evidently hoped to be somewhat more successful with item 27. She correctly related the amount of money being spent to the inflationary boom and the effect of taxes on control of money. She then apparently did some thinking about the consequences of item 28 but did not reveal it. The return to item 26 revealed some little knowledge about the effects of reserves, but there was confusion about the exact relationship. The return to item 28 appeared to bring in the selection of an answer on the basis of a "feeling" rather than clear-cut reasoning. Although she answered two of the items correctly, there is little economy of effort in the problem-solving and little confidence in the accuracy of the solutions.

James S. (Score 2): (Read the statements.) "In other words, the OPA and such.

(Read the directions.) "Taken for granted they're going to control the boom.

(Read item 26. Re-read item 26.) "That would be inconsistent.

(Read item 27.) "That would be inconsistent, because you can't have too great a boom as long as you have taxes, at least in my interpretation of boom – although if taxes go up, prices go up – no, I'll stick to my answer.

(Read item 28.) "Consistent – however, I think I need more subject-matter background to tell how I thought it out – more of a guess – don't think inconsistent, so put consistent."

In this example, the student translated the problem into something much more closely related to his own experiences – the OPA. This method of altering the material of the problem is an essential first step for many of the students. This student also found it necessary to limit the problem by assuming that the boom was to be controlled. He gave no evidence as to his basis for answering item 26. In item 27 there is evidence of doubt, although he adhered to his original decision. Here he related rise in prices to rise in taxes – it is not clear whether he rejects this relationship or not by the "No." Perhaps the vagueness in answering item 27 was the result of his limited knowledge of the field. In item 28 he selected an answer and definitely labeled it a guess. It is interesting to note the mention of lack of subject-matter background as a reason for inability to tell about the reasoning process.

David F. (Score 3): "Will read the statement. (Read the statement and the directions.) Statement of possible policy. See if the suggestions are consistent or inconsistent with the policy.

(Read item 26.) "If they did that, what happens? – Possibility that the banks would crash, so it's inconsistent.

(Read item 27.) "People would have more money to spend, prices would go up, so inconsistent.

(Read item 28.) "Intuitively, I feel that 28 is also inconsistent – can I find a reason – if they do, stocks will go and federal reserve banks, no, inconsistent. Lot of hazy ideas – don't know enough about federal reserve banks or securities in the open market to definitely say inconsistent."

David was a student who stuttered a great deal. This stuttering appeared to get worse when he attempted to describe his problem-solving to the interviewer, but when he was "thinking aloud" as he worked through the problem, there was no sign of speech difficulty. In this example, he restated the directions in such a way as to clarify for himself what the problem involved. He apparently did a great deal of his thinking by asking and answering his own questions. He answered all three items correctly but approached them as involving three independent questions. Thus, in item 26 he related the reduction of reserves to the possibility of bank crashes. This enabled him to answer the item correctly but did not bring into focus the effect of less extreme reductions in the reserve. In item 27 he related reduction in taxes to increases in money available for spending and the consequent rise in prices. Here, without stating it, the student implied that rise in prices is related to an inflationary boom. The student "intuitively" determined that item 28 is inconsistent and then searched for a reason. (This was a characteristic method for many of the students.) He explored one possible consequence of the buying of securities by the federal reserve bank and then rejected it. Although this report on process of problem-solving is somewhat incomplete, it gives a fair idea of how the student attacked the particular problem.

Dora Z. (Score 2): (Read the statement and the directions – emphasizing the key words.)

(Read item 26.) "Lower the reserve, raise the amount of money in circulation – if you raise the money in circulation – inconsistent. By raising the money in circulation you don't control a boom.

(Read item 27.) "Also inconsistent for the same reason.

(Read item 28.) "Open market — think what the open market is. Think would take money out of circulation, therefore would be consistent."

In her reading of the statements and the directions, this student very quickly focused attention on what she considered to be the key words or ideas. She managed to reduce the three items to a single problem by relating the amount of money in circulation to the control of the inflationary boom. In each case she attempted to determine how the amount of money in circulation would be affected by each of the items. Although the report is not complete and it is not clear how item 27 was answered or what she thought the open market is, a rather high order of problem-solving is evident. The ability to reduce three items to a single problem and attack it on the basis of a single rule or principle would appear to be evidence of a very efficient method of dealing with the material. This would seen to be a good method for getting to the heart of a problem and is likely (if the correct elements are selected) to produce correct solutions. In the present instance, however, the student was unable to see the relationship between the purchase of securities on the open market by the federal reserve banks and the amount of money in circulations.

Comments on Problem 3 and the reports. – In this problem the student is called upon to know the meaning of certain key terms such as "inflationary boom," "reserves," "open market." In addition, he must recognize that the problem is not one of deciding whether or not the boom should be controlled but one of determining what is or is not consistent with the policy of controlling a boom. The problem may be attacked by an attempt to remember the exact way in which each of the items might have been discussed in a class or a textbook or by an attempt to work out some general ideas of how an inflationary boom operates and the relation of these ideas to each of the items. Thus, it is possible to relate the inflationary boom to the amount of money in circulation and then to determine the consequences of each of the items in terms of amount of money in circulation. A number of the students had this principle in mind, but only one seemed to be able to follow through on it consistently.

This problem and the reports on the problem-solving are of value in revealing a number of things:

1. The extent to which the same directions may be misleading to some students while completely clear to others. John was evidently unable to determine what he was required to do, and Mary had great difficulty in determining the requirements of the problem.

2. Some students find it necessary to modify the problem or to delimit it before proceeding to a solution. This is well exemplified in James's report.

3. Some students have difficulty in organizing their thought in any systematic way. This may be seen in Mary's problem-solving.

4. Although it is not frequently apparent from the reports, some students appear to proceed in their problem-solving by asking and answering specific questions. This method of thinking is evident in David's report.

5. When given a number of questions on the same topic, students have difficulty in detecting a single idea which runs through all the items. They proceed to attack each question or item separately and independently rather than to attack all as a group. Only one of the students, Dora, appeared able to attack the questions here on the basis of a central idea.

6. Students apparently find it necessary to protect themselves by frequent assertions that they are unable to remember particular ideas or that they are guessing. Some of the students spent as much time in preparing for possible failure as they did in attacking the problem.

In this chapter we have attempted to show the need for further research on mental processes by both the psychologist and the educator. Such research could do much to improve our methods of studying individual differences and could furnish a useful basis for determining the effectiveness of different educational methods.

A few examples of problems and student reports of problem-solving methods have been included to show some of the possibilities of even relatively crude techniques of research in this field. These problems and protocols rather clearly demonstrate that the variations in products of thought (number of correct answers or solutions) do not adequately reflect the variety of mental processes which students bring to these problems.

The problems and protocols reveal differences in the ways in which individual students approach and solve problems. Chapter ii will discuss some of the difficulties students exhibit in solving a variety of problems and will compare groups of students as well as describe characteristics of individual students as revealed by this type of analysis.

These problems and protocols reveal variations in problems, both in the extent to which students are able to reveal their mental processes and in the extent to which various elements in the problem become sources of difficulty. Some of the differences among problems brought out by this type of analysis will be presented in greater detail in chapter iii of this monograph.

Chapter iv describes an attempt to apply the findings of these investigations to the remediation of the habits of problem-solving exhibited by a group of failing students.

The concluding chapter, v, summarizes the work reported in this monograph, discusses briefly some of the implications of these results, and indicates some of the hypotheses about the nature of the mental processes in problem-solving which might be investigated further.

CHAPTER II

VARIATIONS IN THE PROBLEM-SOLVING CHARACTERISTICS
OF STUDENTS

Values of study of mental processes

Evidence on the problem-solving processes used by specific individuals can be of value to the educator and the psychologist in several ways. Such data may be used to describe individual differences, to predict later behavior, to measure changes as a result of specific and identifiable experiences, and to serve as one basis for development of a program of specialized training.

The results of a study of variations in problem-solving methods can serve as an additional source of evidence in the study of individual differences. Such a study provides a new framework for determining the ways in which individuals differ. Data of this kind are especially valuable if they reveal characteristic mental processes for the individual and if they also help to explain some of the more readily observed behavior of the student. Even though all students in a group arrive at the same products of thought, it would seem desirable to determine whether they differ with respect to the processes of thought involved.

The analysis of the thought-processes in this way may also be of value in predicting the methods a subject will use in attacking new problems. As described more fully later, the subjects involved in this study reveal consistent and distinct patterns of problem-solving behavior for a variety of problems. It would seem possible that the collection of this type of data on a relatively small sample of problems might reveal more about an individual and be of greater predictive value than the results of a large battery of tests analyzed in the conventional manner.

Data of this kind should also be valuable in revealing some of the changes made in students as a result of specific educational or other experiences. Records can be obtained on the problem-solving characteristics of a group of subjects before and after the particular experiences, and the changes in problem-solving behavior determined. Later in this chapter, this type of analysis is applied to the problem-solving behavior of first-year students at time of entrance to the College and again six to eight weeks later. These kinds of data are also used in chapter iv to describe changes attributed to a remedial problem-solving program.

Finally, records of variation in problem-solving characteristics can be of value as a basis for determining the specific kinds of training needed for different types of students. For example, a study of the variations in the problem-solving processes of failing students and of academically successful students may be used as one basis for developing a remedial program for failing students. This use of data is discussed at some length in chapter iv of this monograph. Data on problem-solving processes should also be of value in sensitizing a teacher to the mental characteristics of a group of students entering a specific educational unit.

Limitations on study of mental processes

Although the value of a study of mental processes may be quite apparent, the techniques which may be used are relatively inadequate. In this study, we have asked our students to "think aloud" as they attacked problems. The major limitations on this way of analyzing problem-solving processes may be related, in this study, to the kinds of subjects involved, the types of problems used, and the nature of the interview or experimental situation.

Limitations attributable to the sample of subjects used. − A major difficulty is that the students are naïve psychologically and cannot reveal as much of their thought-processes as might be desired. Only a brief training period with simple mathematical problems was provided to develop some skill in "thinking aloud." The subjects were then presented with a variety of problems and were instructed to try to reveal as much as they could of their thought-processes. It was emphasized that they were not to concern themselves about the accuracy of the answer they obtained. Because the subjects tended to edit the solutions they verbalized, it was often necessary to ask them to retrospect in order to fill in a little more of the detail than was provided by the "thinking aloud." The completeness of the process of problem-solving reported by different individuals varied. Some of the students were able to forget themselves almost completely in the situation. One student in particular gave very complete records, including side remarks to herself which indicated a process of self-questioning when planning an attack on a problem or during the actual manipulation of the elements of the problem.

A few students were almost entirely unable to reveal the processes they employed in the attack on problems. They read the problem, gave the answer almost immediately, but were unable to explain or reveal how they had arrived at such a solution. If pressed, they made up a suitable explanation, but it was evident that the entire process had taken place a little too quickly for them to observe it or to be conscious of it. The majority of the students, however, were able to report a good deal of their method of problem-solving. Clearly, they were not able to give a complete picture of everything that took place, but they were able to report enough to permit one to characterize their methods of problem-solving. It is interesting to note that the characteristics revealed were found to be relatively consistent for a particular student at different times and on different problems.

The students available for this study were all enrolled in the College of the University of Chicago. Since a necessary condition for admission to the College is a certain level of performance on the entrance examinations, the data are based on a relatively homogeneous group of college students. It is quite possible that, if this study had included a greater variety of individuals with different ages, different levels of scholastic aptitude and achievement, etc., other characteristics of problem-solving might have been revealed.

Limitations offered by the problems used in the study. − Another limitation on this study of variations in problem-solving is that only academic-aptitude and achievement-test problems were used. The problems chosen were those in which thought and reasoning, rather than memory of information alone, were necessary for the obtaining of a solution. They were mainly of the recognition type of test question, with multiple-choice and master-list forms predominating. These problems were highly structured and did not allow much opportunity for the introduction of values or for the introduction of a great range of solutions.

Since the process of record-taking was slow and laborious, it was impossible to get records of the attack on a large sample of problems for each student. For each subject, records were obtained on about twenty problems. This limitation may not be serious, since, as the study proceeded, it was found that the records for each student showed a great deal of consistency in the methods of problem-solving employed. At present, it appears likely that six to eight carefully chosen problems could reveal most of the problem-solving characteristics of an individual.

Limitations present in the situation itself. – The conditions of the experimental situation placed limitations on the data obtainable. Since the experiments were conducted on an individual basis, with only one subject and the experimenter present, it seems likely that some of the characteristics of problem-solving described here might not be present in a real examination situation or in an attack on a "real life" problem.

The students worked under much less tension in the experimental situation. They were told that we were not concerned greatly about the accuracy of the answer to the problem and that what we wanted was as much as they could reveal of their method of attacking the problem. It is likely that this emphasis on process rather than product may reveal methods of attacking problems which are somewhat different from those normally used by the subject.

Again, the time allowed for the solution of a problem was unlimited in the experimental situation, whereas in the usual examination situation a time limit is imposed by the student himself or by outside agencies. The experimental situation, however, was not totally without time limits, since the students did impose limits on themselves. One student, for example, rushed through the problems at top speed and omitted several problems. He indicated that in a real examination there just would not have been sufficient time to solve them.

Another limitation imposed by the situation was that the experimenter was always present, and the students were conscious that their words were being recorded. This effect apparently was minimized after the students had been in the situation about ten to fifteen minutes. An attempt was made to record the solutions on a wire recorder, but the students seemed more disturbed by the apparatus than by the presence of the experimenter. With another, later group and with less conspicuous apparatus, the wire recorder was successfully used. This method offers a more complete record and has an additional advantage in that the subject can be left alone while the experimenter is engaged in other activities.

Successful and unsuccessful students

A major task in this study was the simplication, classification, and analysis of results. Verbatim reports were made as the student attacked each problem. These reports were extremely lengthy and specific and were of value primarily as raw data.

The attempts at analysis of the protocols were aided by the first study in this investigation, in which the participating students came from two sharply defined academic-achievement groups. These included six academically successful students with high scores on aptitude tests and grades of A and B on the achievement examinations. At the other extreme were six academically nonsuccessful students with low aptitude scores and grades of D and F on the comprehensive achievement examinations. Each protocol was examined carefully, and an effort was made to list specific character- istics which tentatively seemed of importance in describing the attack, in explaining failure on the problem, or in appraising the quality of the mental processes involved. The characteristics of the extreme groups were then studied to determine consistency within each group as well as differences between the groups. In making this analysis, we realized that differences in academic achievement might possibly be due to factors of motivation, emo- tional imbalance, differences in "native intelligence," or to the amount of studying done by the student. It seems likely, however, that some of the dif- ferences in achievement could be accounted for by differences in methods of attacking problems. This particular hypothesis has been explored in some detail in chapter iv of this report. In discussing differences between the two groups, we have frequently referred to them as successful and unsuccessful problem-solvers. It was our judgment that the differences in their success in problem-solving were as marked as the differences in their academic achievement.

Analyses of the differences in methods of problem-solving between the groups and between the individuals were made in various ways, including at- tempts to fit the data into previously defined classifications, such as that of Dewey (4). However, none of these classifications seemed to summarize ade- quately the specific data obtained in this study. After several attempts at classification of the data, four major headings were selected:

1. Understanding of the nature of the problem
2. Understanding of the ideas contained in the problem
3. General approach to the solution of problems
4. Attitude toward the solution of problems

Each of these categories is discussed in some detail in the following sec- tions.

1. Understanding of the nature of the problem. — By "understanding of the nature of the problem" is meant understanding the kind of problem to be attacked — more or less a clarification of what is involved or required in the problem. In this general area the successful problem-solvers usually differed from the nonsuccessful problem-solvers in two ways: in their abil- ity to start attack on a problem and in their ability to solve the problem in its own terms.

A major difference between the two groups was found in their ability to start the attack on a problem. The successful problem-solvers seemed able to read the directions and the statement of a problem and almost immedi- ately to choose some point at which to begin their attack — some word or phrase on which to begin their process of reasoning. For example, on the problem given in Figure 5, the successful student pulled out the key ideas by saying, "Corporations, competition, individualism, and free enterprise. Corporations just don't go together with competition, individualism, and free enterprise." The nonsuccessful problem-solvers, on the other hand, would read the same statement of the problem and then begin to flounder. They might read and re-read the statement and complain, "I don't understand what it means," or "This doesn't make sense." In general, the non-successful students seem to have established no effective technique for starting the solution. Rarely did they pull out some key word or break the statement into lesser parts which they might find easier to understand.

For each of the following statements, <u>blacken</u>

    answer space 1 if the statement is <u>true</u>;
    answer space 2 if the statement is <u>false</u>.

The growth of corporations in size and influence in America in the last half-century has been part of a trend toward increasing competition, individualism, and free enterprise in economic life.

Figure 5

In many cases the inability of the nonsuccessful problem-solver to begin the solution of the problem resulted from lack of comprehension of the directions. In some cases this lack of comprehension was evidently due to failure to read the directions or to a misunderstanding of terms or phrases in the directions. It was noted that many of the nonsuccessful problem-solvers "skipped" the directions in whole or in part. Frequently, failure to read the directions seemed to be part of an effort to hasten the problem-solving and to save time. The successful problem-solvers did a certain amount of shortening of the directions, but it was done in a different manner. Thus, they would omit repeated phrases or scan the directions in such a way as to select ideas. In their shortening of directions, they lost none of the essence, while the nonsuccessful problem-solvers seemed to skip indiscriminately. For the successful students, this condensing or shortening seemed to bring the major elements into focus.

Understanding of the terms in the directions was another factor affecting success or failure in beginning the attack on a problem. The nonsuccessful problem-solvers misunderstood terms or phrases and were frequently confused about the requirements of the problem. Under similar circumstances, the successful problem-solvers made an assumption as to the possible meaning of a term or attempted to use some other clue present in the problem as a basis for beginning their attack.

The two groups differed considerably in <u>their ability to solve the problem as presented.</u> The nonsuccessful student would frequently present an acceptable or correct solution to the problem he had attacked, but this problem was not the one he had been asked to solve. Failure to attack the problem as posed was due, in some instances, to a neglected or misinterpreted term in the directions. In other instances it resulted from a failure to keep the directions in mind as the problem was being solved. Thus, in one problem which presented a statement and three comments on the statement, the student was directed to choose the one comment which showed best understanding of the subject discussed in the statement. Many of the nonsuccessful students lost sight of these directions as they proceeded with the solution of the problem and chose the comment which most nearly expressed the same ideas as the statement. For the problem they were solving, they had achieved a good solution, but for the problem originally posed, they had achieved a poor solution. When their attention was called to the directions for the problem, these students were usually able to determine the correct solution.

Again, we found the nonsuccessful student presenting a solution for a different-from-the-intended problem as a result of failure to read the directions completely, or of misreading or misinterpreting them. The misinterpretation was not due, in most instances, to lack of understanding of the actual terms or phrases in the directions but rather to a very superficial perusal of them. In other words, although the directions were not comprehended by the student, it was clear that he was capable of understanding them if he read them with sufficient care.

2. Understanding of the ideas contained in the problem. — By this we mean possession of the basic information necessary for the solution to a problem as well as the ability to bring this knowledge to bear in attacking the problem.

In this general area the outstanding difference between the successful and the nonsuccessful problem-solvers was not, as might have been expected, a difference in the amount of relevant knowledge possessed by the two groups. The major difference was in the extent to which the two groups could bring the relevant knowledge they possessed to bear on the problem. Often the nonsuccessful students had within their grasp all the background and technical information necessary for the solution of a problem but were unable to apply the knowledge to the problem. One student, for instance, was given a complex problem involving a set of observations and requiring judgment about a list of possible conclusions to be drawn from the observations. After reading the problem, the student felt that she "just didn't have enough information to solve it." When the experimenter prodded, encouraged, and questioned her further, the student discovered that she did possess the necessary information. She finally solved the problem correctly, much to her surprise.

The nonsuccessful students seemed unable to realize fully the implications of the ideas of the problem. For example, when these students were asked a question concerning "corporate enterprise in America," they were confused and seemed unable to answer the question. If, however, as a result of a series of questions by the experimenter, they came to realize that the Ford Motor Company or some other specific corporation could be considered an example of "corporate enterprise," they were able to deal adequately with the question posed. On a problem dealing with methods for the control of inflation, they would say, "We haven't studied that yet," or "I don't know about that." When, however, they were questioned about specific wartime controls, they seemed fully aware of the purpose of those restrictions. After these specific questions they appeared to have little difficulty in putting the various pieces of information together and correctly solved the problem. They had gained no information but had acquired a new orientation to the problem. Apparently, they were unable to deal with or to comprehend ideas in the form presented in the problem.

The unsuccessful problem-solvers had difficulty in relating their read-

ings and lecture notes to the problem if the problem material was presented in a form different from the form they had encountered in their studying.
For instance, one student had great difficulty with a genetics problem because of changes in the symbols used. In the problems she had worked at
home, the recessive individuals were represented by black symbols and the
dominant by white, whereas in the examination this symbolism was reversed.
In a problem dealing with state rights, the nonsuccessful students were reluctant to attack the problem, saying they didn't know what state rights were.
But, if asked to tell some of the rights of states or if asked to contrast state
rights with the rights of the federal government, they could proceed with the
solution to the problem. This ability to put relevant knowledge to use is apparently related to the individual's self-confidence.

It seemed, then, that the ideas which the nonsuccessful problem-solvers
possessed were huge, unwieldy things, figuratively capable of fitting into only one particular space – that in which they had originally been framed. The
ideas of the successful problem-solvers, in contrast, were many-faceted
things which could be turned this way and that, expanded or contracted, and
made to fit the space in which they were needed.

In some few instances, the students had difficulty using the relevant
knowledge at their command, due to the presence of totally unfamiliar or
highly abstract terms or ideas. Under such circumstances, the successful
problem-solvers attempted to translate the difficult and abstract terms of
the problem into simpler, more concrete, or more familiar terms. Frequently they made tentative assumptions about the meaning of unfamiliar
terms, even though they recognized that some of these assumptions were
probably not entirely correct. In contrast, the nonsuccessful problem-solvers
quickly gave up and prepared to "go on to the next problem." Frequently the
successful problem-solvers would substitute an illustration or example for
a difficult or vague concept and then think in terms of these illustrations
and examples. This kind of thinking appeared to help them solve the problem. In contrast, the nonsuccessful problem-solvers treated vague or unfamiliar concepts as given and appeared unable to do anything further with
them.

3. General approach to the solution of problems. – By this we mean the
procedure of the student during his attack on a problem. The analysis of the
protocols indicates that the successful and the nonsuccessful problem-
solvers differ in three general respects in their approach to the solution of
problems. These are: extent of thought about the problem, care and system
in thinking about the problem, and ability to follow through on a process of
reasoning.

---

123. Give the reasons which would have influenced a typical
Virginia tobacco farmer to support the ratification of the
Constitution in 1788, and the reasons which would have
influenced him to oppose the ratification.

Figure 6

The major difference between the successful and the nonsuccessful
problem-solvers in their extent of thought about the problem was in the de-

gree to which their approach to the problem might be characterized as active or passive. Contrast the solutions to the problem presented in Figure 6.

George H: "Well, uh, I have to read the statement over, I haven't had any history for three years, and, uh, 'Give the reasons which would have influenced the typical Virginia tobacco farmer to support the ratification of the Constitution in 1788 and reasons which would have influenced him to oppose ratification.' Well, uh, to tell the truth I never had anything on the reasons of a Virginia tobacco farmer and at present I couldn't think of any."

Ralph R: (Reads the statement of the problem.) "Tobacco farmers are quite wealthy, I imagine. He has to pay, ratification of the Constitution, well, what rights did the Constitution give him? Well, starting at the end, well, from the standpoint of money, which one would be more to his advantage? Well, prior to the Revolutionary War, he would have to pay taxes to England, but that isn't applying here. Support ratification of the Constitution. Well, as any other citizen of the colonies, I suppose he would approve of the Constitution, but as a Virginia tobacco planter, well, I think he would approve of it for patriotic reasons, and from the standpoint of money he wouldn't have to ship his tobacco to England or anything. Well, he wouldn't have to pay the taxes."

George probably has almost as much real knowledge about the Virginia tobacco farmer as Ralph. However, Ralph keeps working with what is given until he is able to give some semblance of a solution.

The successful problem-solvers would read the statement of the problem and then set up their own hypothesis as to the correct solution, or, where the nature of the problem made this an impossibility, they would set up the criteria which the correct answer must fulfil. Where the problem contained unfamiliar terms, the successful problem-solvers would make an assumption with regard to their meaning and proceed with a solution based on these assumptions.

In contrast, the nonsuccessful problem-solvers were almost completely passive in their thinking about the problem. They gave little time to a consideration of the problem, selecting an answer on the basis of very few clues or on superficial considerations. There was a definite tendency on the part of these students to select an answer on the basis of "impression" or "feelings" about which choice might be correct. They attempted to remember the solution to a similar problem rather than solving each new problem independently. They used a negative approach — that of selecting one answer because none of the others appeared attractive. The nonsuccessful problem-solvers might look at the choice of answers and select one purely on a guesswork basis. One student when in doubt always chose answer B, because on one test he had noticed that a good many of the answers had been marked in answer space B. Again, the nonsuccessful problem-solvers might make little or no attempt to reason about a problem because of lack of confidence in their knowledge of the material.

There was a noticeable difference between the successful and the nonsuccessful problem-solvers in their care and system in thinking about the problem. As might be expected, the successful problem-solvers were careful and systematic in their method of attack on the problem. They seemed to take the problem as given and reorganize it to simplify it, pulling out the key terms or ideas, or breaking the problem into simpler subproblems, in order to gain an understanding of the material. They attempted to eliminate some of the given answers as clearly incorrect. They then attempted to determine which of the remaining answers was correct, apparently finding it more efficient to decide between one of two or three choices, than one of five. Further, they attempted to deal with each part of the problem separately, if the whole were too complex for easy manipulation.

The nonsuccessful problem-solvers, on the other hand, started the problem with no apparent plan for solution, more or less plunging in, not knowing what was to come next. They jumped from one part of the problem to another, giving insufficient consideration to any one part to enable them to find a beginning point of attack. They would attack the problem as a whole, reading the directions, the statement of the problem, and the alternatives again and again, searching for some clue to the solution. The nonsuccessful problem-solvers neglected to consider important details in the solution or were extremely careless in considering these details. They were easily sidetracked by external considerations − some word might suggest a book they had read or an interesting incident, and their thoughts would go off on this tangent, coming back to the problem at hand only with considerable difficulty.

The successful and the nonsuccessful problem-solvers were also found to differ in the method by which they justified their selection of an answer. The successful problem-solvers would consider each alternative answer as they came to it, reasoning to decide whether or not it was a possible answer. The nonsuccessful problem-solvers would select one of the choices offered, seemingly on the basis of impression or feeling as to which answer "seemed right." They then attempted to find some justification for this choice, frequently offering some trivial or irrelevant point as a defense for their selection of an answer.

A further point of difference between the successful and the nonsuccessful problem-solvers was evident in their ability to follow through on a process of reasoning. The nonsuccessful problem-solvers might begin their attack on a problem in much the same way as the successful problem-solvers, carry their reasoning part way through to completion, and then give up. They would start to solve the problem with a definite plan for the solution in mind, but would then lose sight of the original plan as difficulties were encountered and never return to it. If they had carried it through, the plan probably would have led to a successful solution. The nonsuccessful problem-solvers occasionally elaborated a hypothesis as to the correct solution or set up criteria that the correct solution must fulfil, just as the successful problem-solvers did, but then neglected to apply this reasoning to the selection of a final answer.

4. Attitude toward the solution of problems. − By "attitude" the writers mean the emotions, values, and prejudices of the student as they are involved in the attack on problems. These attitudinal characteristics are observable in the student's reactions to the form and content of the problem. The attitude of the student toward the solution of problems and the nature of the problem material was found to be another point of differentiation between the successful and the nonsuccessful students. In many instances, it was an

important factor in determining the success of the problem-solving. It was possible to identify at least three distinct kinds of attitudes: attitude toward reasoning, confidence in ability to solve problems, and introduction of personal considerations into the solution of problems.

The writers found that many of the nonsuccessful problem-solvers had difficulty because of their attitude toward reasoning. These students were inclined to take the view that, in solving problems, reasoning is of little value and that either one knows the answer to a problem at once or one does not. These students would look at a problem and quickly decide that they could or could not solve it. They appeared to make such judgments largely on the basis of whether or not they thought they possessed all the necessary information. Unlike the successful students, they could see no way of manipulating the parts of the problem if they were not certain of their knowledge of the subject. They could not see problems as things to be broken down into subproblems, nor were they willing to make assumptions to fill gaps in their information. Many of the students who refused to attempt problems because they felt they did not know the answer did, in reality, have sufficient information. One student in particular, after refusing to attempt a problem in reasoning which she felt was quite beyond her, was persuaded to attack it piece by piece, just to see how far she could get. She found that, following this piecemeal approach, she was quite capable of solving the problem.

The nonsuccessful students had little confidence in their ability to solve the problems. They were easily discouraged and made little or no attempt to attack problems which appeared complex or abstract. The format of the problem was sufficient to discourage them from attempting any attack. Thus, many of them would look at a complex graph or table of figures in the problem and quit at once. Sometimes they would make a superficial attempt to reason through a problem and then just give up and guess, for no apparent reason. Lack of confidence in their ability to solve problems extended to lack of confidence in the correctness of the solution they had obtained. They went back to the problem and changed their answer over and over again. Sometimes they were unable to come to a definite conclusion or to decide between one or two alternatives. These students indicated that in a test they would put down an answer just on the chance it would earn an extra point but that, in the interview situation, this was not necessary, and they were willing to leave the decision unmade.

Again, there was a difference between the successful and the nonsuccessful problem-solvers in the frequency with which they introduced personal considerations into their problem-solving. The nonsuccessful problem-solvers had difficulty in maintaining an objective attitude in certain problems because their personal opinions played such an important role. Thus, although the directions to the problem might clearly state, "Assume the statements are true," the student was unable to sufficiently divorce his personal convictions from the problem to enable him to solve it objectively. Some of the students also had difficulty in differentiating between correct answers and answers that seemed desirable on the basis of their personal value patterns. For example, in a syllogistic problem where the two premises are given and the student is to choose the logical conclusion, one student reported, "Answer A is the one that logically follows, but C is the one I believe, so I take C."

31

This difficulty in remaining objective and staying with the central problem when value considerations are involved is well illustrated in the exercise given in Figure 7.

DIRECTIONS: One sentence in each of the following paragraphs has been deliberately spoiled – by mistakes in grammar, by transposing the order of words, by adding unnecessary words or by omitting essential words, by trite expressions and inappropriate figures of speech, by changing tenses, by violations of parallel construction, by vagueness in the reference of pronouns, and the like. Since no sentence in ordinary journalistic writing is perfect, you may dislike more than one sentence in each paragraph, but it should be possible to distinguish deliberately spoiled sentences from sentences which are acceptable by ordinary standards. You are to blacken one answer space for each paragraph corresponding to the worst sentence in that paragraph.

106. A – I am deeply concerned about the bill introduced by Representative Wadsworth and Senator Gurney to establish universal compulsory military training.
B – I feel it is my duty to challenge the wisdom of this bill, not only because I am a student of social and political questions, but I have made a special study of this particular question for nearly fifty years.
C – I believe that Congress is interested in the opinion of citizens, and especially in the opinion of those who have been careful students of the problems which come before Congress.

Figure 7

Fred C: (Read each of the alternatives.) "I think alternative C shows not only exaggerated self-opinion but is neglecting the fact that our representatives have ability to handle the problem. For them to act is one thing, and for them to be acted on is another."

In this exercise Fred C. completely lost sight of the real problem — selecting the sentence which is the worst from the standpoint of grammar — and converted it into a problem involving the duties and responsibilities of congressmen.

The nonsuccessful students were distracted by many external considerations, such as opinions of the course, the instructors, the examination, etc. One student became so incensed over the difficulty of a particular question that she went on to rant against her instructors and the examinations. She then told of her plan for transferring to another school and never did get back to the solution of the problem.

Individual differences

The four major areas described above have been discussed in terms of the characteristics of groups of students, principally in terms of academically successful and nonsuccessful students. In the discussion to follow, it is planned to indicate how descriptions of individual students may be made in terms of these same four major areas. The frequency and the seriousness with which difficulties classified under these four headings may occur in their problem-solving differ considerably from individual to individual. Naturally, the clarity with which various difficulties are revealed and the extent to which each of the characteristics affects the success of the problem-solving are, to a large extent, determined by the nature of the problems used.

Several typical descriptions of the problem-solving characteristics of students entering the first year of the College of the University of Chicago follow. It is hoped that these descriptions will give the reader some idea as to the nature of the data which may be obtained and presented in studies of the mental processes of individual students.

Problem-solving report of Louis S.

1. Understanding of the nature of the problem. – A major factor in this student's lack of understanding of the problem is the fact that he misreads and misinterprets directions. This results, in many instances, in his attempting to solve an entirely different problem from the one posed. In a figure analogy problem, in which the student is directed to select a figure having certain properties, Louis, instead of proceeding according to the directions, described how each of the alternative answers might have been derived from the initial figure. He rarely focuses attention on the essential parts of the directions, seemingly reading them as an unimportant part of his attack on the problem.

2. Understanding of the ideas contained in the problem. – Louis deals almost entirely with the terms as given in the problem, making no attempt to define these terms or to translate them into more familiar terms related to his own experience. He appears to have a somewhat limited technical vocabulary, and this proves to be a definite handicap to his problem-solving. During the problem-solving interview, he wrote down a good many words he planned to look up later in his dictionary. He is much disturbed by the fact that an addition or omission of one or two words in the problem changes the entire meaning of the problem.

3. General approach to the solution of problems. – Louis seems to do little independent thinking in arriving at a solution, relying rather on the choices the examiner supplies. He selects an answer and attempts to justify it, rather than thinking through to the solution and then selecting an answer. Many times he does not know how or where to begin to attack the problem. For example, after fumbling with one problem for some time, he finally said, "Don't see it. Don't know what to do here, not even thinking, only thinking of thinking. Don't know where to begin," and dropped the problem. He frequently chooses the answer on the basis of some general, superficial impression – the answer that "seems right."

4. Attitude toward the solution of problems. – Louis feels that he does not have an adequate background with which to attack certain problems, and he refuses to attempt the solution of these problems. He indicated that he believes it is unfair to guess at an answer. He will not select an answer unless he feels that he has a basis for his choice. (This basis may at times be quite flimsy.) When an answer is chosen, it is usually given in a rather positive and assured manner. He takes the attitude that one does or does not

know the answer, and he makes little attempt to reason through to a solution. Another source of considerable difficulty for this student is that he cannot divorce his personal values from the problems he is solving and seems unable to maintain an objective attitude. Thus, he chooses an answer "that would be not only logic, but also using my interpretation of equity."

5. Comments. – In general, Louis has great difficulty in his problem-solving because he does little in the way of logical or systematic thinking. He is careless in his analysis of the problems and seems to have no adequate method for attacking certain problems. His personal values and emotional considerations frequently lead him astray.

Problem-solving report of Jane C.

1. Understanding of the nature of the problem. – Jane C. frequently begins the attack on a problem without knowing exactly what she is to do, not because she is unable to comprehend the directions, but because she has not taken the time or trouble to understand fully. For example, on one problem she began her attack in this manner, "Will forget about the directions and read the two statements." She then read the statements and had to go back to read the directions to determine what she was expected to do. On other problems she may ignore the directions and go on to discover in the middle of her attack that she is not doing it correctly. She will then go back to the directions and may finally arrive at a correct solution.

2. Understanding of the ideas contained in the problem. – Jane gives some evidence that she understands the ideas involved in the problem when she takes the necessary time and care for this understanding.

3. General approach to the solution of problems. – Jane is inconsistent in her method of problem-solving. She may attack one problem hurriedly, with little consideration, and will then go to great lengths in her care and system in thinking on other problems. She may set up a hypothesis or possible answer, which she checks against the alternatives supplied in the test. At times she possesses all the characteristics of the most successful problem-solvers we have observed, but at other times her problem-solving techniques are extremely careless and poor. She seems to do everything hurriedly, in a constant race against time, although time was not stressed in the interview situation.

4. Attitude toward the solution of problems. – She may look at a problem and decide that it is beyond her understanding without making a serious attempt to comprehend it. She also gives evidence of doubting her own capabilities. A typical reaction was the following, "Wouldn't do anything with this. Just say couldn't do it. Never had anything like this. Don't know the symbols. Not even thinking. Suppose that's bad, but -----" When she does attack a problem, however, she usually does an excellent job. She seems to have a particular fear of, or dislike for, mathematics problems (due, perhaps, to a lack of basic knowledge) and is extremely reluctant to attack these problems. She is much more sure of herself in English and the humanities and is more willing to try to attack these problems.

5. Comments. – Jane works spasmodically in fits and starts, presenting an extremely inconsistent approach to problem-solving. Usually, she does not attack problems systematically and carefully. However, she appears to be able to reason through problems very well when she is so inclined.

Problem-solving report of Fern G.

1. Understanding of the nature of the problem. — Fern, who reads very quickly, appears to emphasize the important points in the directions and in the statement of the problem by pronouncing key words very emphatically and by scanning the material and selecting the key words. She has little difficulty in comprehending what she is to do and in holding the requirements of the problem in mind as she works through it.

2. Understanding of the ideas contained in the problem. — She seems to understand and is able to work with the content of most of the problems and has little difficulty with the terminology employed. She relates abstract statements to specific examples in her experience.

3. General approach to the solution of problems. — It appeared to be difficult for Fern to convey to us the methods she used in problem-solving. She solved problems rapidly and with great assurance, but she did not seem to be able to verbalize how she did it. Many times she would read through the problem and answer it almost immediately. When asked how she had determined the answer, she replied, in one instance, "Just when I came to it I knew it was the right answer."

There was some evidence that she developed a possible hypothesis as to the correct solution as she read through a problem for the first time. She then proceeded to inspect the alternative answers given in the problem to find the one that satisfied her hypothesis. If she was uncertain about some of the terms or ideas, she would set up assumptions as to what these might be and would then go on with her reasoning. If she was not certain of an answer, she would eliminate several of the choices and then confine her reasoning to the remaining alternatives. She worked actively with any of the clues given in the problem.

4. Attitude toward the solution of problems. — To a large extent, Fern accepts problems as capable of solution through reasoning. A typical reaction was, "Know absolutely nothing about this, but suppose from reasoning can get something." She then went on to a satisfactory attack on the problem. Where her knowledge of the subject matter is inadequate, she makes every effort to think through to a solution. However, when she was convinced that she lacked the necessary knowledge, she refused to attempt the problem. She was somewhat troubled when presented with problems she had worked at an earlier date, in that she could not forget the solution she had arrived at previously,

5. Comments. — Fern is an excellent problem-solver who works so rapidly as to have difficulty in expressing the methods of reasoning used. She gave some evidence of using a logical and methodical approach.

Problem-solving report of Nancy R.

1. Understanding of the nature of the problem. — Nancy seems to have little difficulty understanding the nature of a problem. However, if the problem is exceedingly complex or if the solution is not immediately apparent, she becomes so involved in the details of the problem that she loses sight of the end she is seeking. As she reads the directions, she sometimes restates them in her own words, picking out the relevant ideas and determining exactly what she is to look for.

2. Understanding of the ideas involved in the solution of a problem. — She seems to have little difficulty understanding the ideas involved. When she is uncertain about a term used or has difficulty visualizing a situation, she seems to try to relate it to a concrete example or to establish a mental picture in order to clarify the situation for herself. She presents a particularly good example of one who can relate her knowledge and experiences to the problem at hand.

3. General approach to the solution of problems. — Nancy is continually asking herself questions about the problem as she proceeds with the attack. She seems to answer these questions and then to go ahead on the basis of the answers and assumptions she has made. If she cannot attack the problem as a whole, she breaks it into parts and attacks each part separately. Her habit of questioning the various parts of a problem seems to be the directing influence in her ability to break down a problem. In a few instances, Nancy appeared to select an answer only because it "seemed" best, with no apparent reasoning involved.

4. Attitude toward the solution of problems. — She expresses some feelings of inferiority regarding her ability to attack certain problems. A typical reaction in a problem dealing with the laws of exponents was, "Wonder if I remember this. $a^n b^n = (ab)^n$. This was one of our theorems, wasn't it? Can't use that because the converse. What is given in the product when you first learn coefficients? Darn it, Nancy, you should know this. Coefficients. How did they do this? I can't remember at all." She usually makes some attempt to find an answer for each problem. She makes a great effort to explore her knowledge about a subject to determine what is relevant to each problem.

5. Comments. — Nancy seemed to have little difficulty in the experimental situation and to be quite at home in introspecting, or "thinking aloud." The interviewer thought it quite likely that she uses this method habitually. If this is true, one wonders what effect it has on her methods of study. She is a fairly good problem-solver, making excellent use of a limited amount of knowledge and doing very well in breaking problems into manageable proportions.

Differences revealed

The individual differences revealed by these reports cannot be inferred from the test scores that students make. The variations in the understanding of a problem, the extent to which the student possesses and can use relevant information, the general approach to the solution of problems, and the student's attitude when solving problems reveal much about the student. There is a sufficient amount of consistency in the data on each student to indicate that the problem-solving interview can get at habitual behavior.

It is realized that much must be done to develop the techniques of securing evidence on, and describing, the individual's problem-solving characteristics. There is the problem of how to secure the data under conditions which will most nearly reveal the student's usual way of approaching problems. The techniques of describing and characterizing an individual's problem-solving are still extremely awkward and subjective. However, even these crude reports on problem-solving reveal four students who differ greatly. Each student seems to need quite a different kind of instruction, and each student probably studies and learns in quite a different way.

In chapter iv we report the use of this technique as a basis for remedial work with failing students in the College of the University of Chicago. If these techniques can be developed so that they result in an objective picture of the individual's mental processes, they might very well serve as the basis for a distinct approach to the measurement of intelligence or aptitude. In addition, these techniques should serve for the measurement of many of the educational changes which are too subtle for the usual test of achievement to distinguish.

Group characteristics

The foregoing description of methods of problem-solving has been concerned primarily with extreme students and individual students. These data would be of little value, however, in describing or analyzing the methods of problem-solving used by the large majority of college students; nor do these data indicate the ways in which groups of students change in their problem-solving methods as they progress through college. In an attempt to secure data on the problem-solving of the more typical college student, an investigation was conducted on a small group of students (27) entering the first year of the College of the University of Chicago in January, 1946. These students were observed twice, once within their first three weeks in the College, and again six to eight weeks later.

First observation. — The investigation was conducted in the same manner as the original study. The students were interviewed individually. They were presented with a variety of examination problems and were directed to think aloud as they attempted to solve the problems. They were informed that the interviewer was interested primarily in the way they thought, rather than in the accuracy of their solutions. In this particular group, only three individuals seemed somewhat disconcerted by the requirements of the situation, while one student, Nancy R., whose individual report is given above, presented some evidence that "thinking aloud" is the typical way in which she attacks problems.

It is difficult to report on the problem-solving of this group of students. They, for the most part, did not exhibit to so great a degree the characteristics noted in the extreme students. The writers find it difficult to express in words the complex processes of problem-solving — it is much like trying to describe a dance or an involved musical composition. Again, the problems involved are examination problems and are, therefore, somewhat artificial. The writers are of the opinion, however, that such problems give the student an opportunity to exhibit his best problem-solving. We believe that most of the difficulties exhibited by the students on these problems are greatly accentuated when they are required to solve "real-life" problems which are personal, urgent, and infinitely more complex.

In thinking about the problem-solving of this typical college group, it is possible to analogize it to the variations in muscular co-ordination, which are so much more readily observed than thought-processes. In a rough way, it is possible to classify most students, on the basis of their problem-solving, into four groups which are paralleled by four levels of muscular co-ordination. A few gifted individuals, like the successful students previously described, seem to move with an effortless grace — every movement seems to be maximally effective in achieving a desired end. In the field of problem-

37

solving, none of the students in the entering class exhibited this highest order of economy and effectiveness of thought in the initial analysis.

Another group of less gifted individuals has some difficulty in muscular
co-ordination. While not very great, these difficulties make for some awk-
wardness and wasted motion. These individuals move toward their goal, but
not with maximum economy. This type of problem-solving behavior was exhibited by two of the students in the entering class in the initial analysis (2
of 27).

Persons in still a third group move toward their goals, but only after a
great deal of lost motion. These individuals have little in the way of a plan,
seem to release much energy, make many muscular movements quite unre-
lated to the end to be attained, and appear to reach their goal more by chance
than by plan. In the first analysis, most of the students in the entering group
exhibited this type of problem-solving (20 of 27).

The poorest group in muscular co-ordination is composed of individuals
who are unable to see a goal or to keep it in mind long enough to achieve it.
Members of this group seem to waste all but a tiny fraction of the muscular
energy expended and make motions in every direction without apparent reason. They practically never attain the end set before them. It is as though
one directed an individual to walk out of a room and then observed him going
in every direction except toward the door. Several of the students in the entering group (5 of 27) demonstrated this type of problem-solving behavior
in the first interview session.

Some of the major sources of difficulty in the problem-solving of this
typical group of students which were demonstrated at the first analysis can
be classified under five points:

1. Many of the students have great difficulty in ascertaining what they
are required to do. They do not fully comprehend the nature of the problem
and do not quite see how to proceed. To a large extent, this difficulty results from the speed and carelessness with which they read and the inadequate attention they give to the directions. In class these students would
probably attempt to solve problems with very little notion of what the problem really is, as they rarely stop to define a task before beginning it.

2. Another major source of difficulty for these students is their lack of
objectivity in dealing with problems. Each problem takes on an emotional
coloring which handicaps them rather severely. Their dislike for various
subject fields, their feelings of inadequacy, their fear of problems which
look too difficult and complex, their personal and social values, and their
lack of success in previous efforts — all these emotional factors lead them
to refuse to attempt certain problems or to give up the attack on a problem
after relatively little consideration. These emotional aspects of problem-
solving are serious and must be overcome if the individual is to do thinking and problem-solving anywhere near the level of which he is capable.

3. Another source of difficulty is the inability of the student to reason
logically and systematically. Many of these students seem to grope blindly
toward a solution. Their problem-solving is characterized by feelings,
hunches, and guesses. They are rarely confident of the solution they have
reached and are not at all clear how they arrived at it.

4. Another frequent source of difficulty is inability to complete a chain
of reasoning. The student starts very nicely and is able to go through several steps in the reasoning process. Then, for some unknown reason, he is

unable to continue with the implications of the reasoning process he has started. These individuals do not appear to be able to follow through a chain of reasoning which has any complexity.

5. A frequent source of difficulty in the students' attacks on the particular problems presented was lack of necessary subject-matter knowledge. This can probably be more easily remedied than any of the preceding four difficulties.

Later observation. — In the second problem-solving interview (six to eight weeks after the first), the same procedures were used as in the first interview. The students were again asked to solve some of the problems presented at the first interview and, in addition, were given new problems to attack. Some of the major changes observed in the group were as follows:

1. They were more careful and systematic in their attack. Where formerly they had attacked many of the problems in a haphazard fashion, they now took more time and made a more directed effort toward solving the problem. If they were unable to work with the problem as a whole, they would begin on a part of it. They had less difficulty determining just what they were required to do in a particular problem.

2. They had increased confidence in their ability to solve problems and attacked a larger proportion of problems than they had at the first interview.

3. They did more thinking about each problem, spending more time developing a solution. They tended to select an answer less on the basis of impression or feeling and more on the basis of detailed reasoning.

4. They had, of course, increased knowledge of subject matter. This undoubtedly was a great influence on the other changes observed.

It was interesting to note that there was little change in their objectivity in dealing with a problem. They still evidenced dislike for particular subject fields and still introduced personal considerations into their problem-solving. In only one or two instances was there a marked change from an extremely emotional approach to problem-solving to a very objective one. It was expected, of course, that students would show increased knowledge of subject matter after the lapse of time. Since this was their second appearance in the experimental situation, they were probably somewhat more assured and confident. The other changes that took place and the degree of change in each instance have implications for further study.

It would seem, therefore, that an analysis of the problem-solving of individuals in a typical college group can be made, that this analysis will show some of the characteristics recognizable in extreme groups of college students (although usually to a lesser degree), and that it is possible to determine some of the changes that take place in the problem-solving of college students at intervals in their college career.

Summary

In this chapter on variations of problem-solving in students, the writers have attempted to show that variations can be shown to exist through use of the technique of asking students to solve problems as they "think aloud," that most of the problem-solving characteristics can be classified in four major areas, and that these classifications can be used to differentiate groups of students and individual students. The problem-solving characteristics of a typical group of entering students were analyzed, and the degree to which these characteristics change over a six- to eight-week interval was investigated.

CHAPTER III

VARIATIONS IN PROBLEMS AS REVEALED BY
PROBLEM-SOLVING INVESTIGATIONS

In chapter ii some of the differences in the problem-solving characteristics of college students were described. There the emphasis was on how
students differ in their methods of attack on a series of problems. By-prod-
ucts of this type of investigation are the data secured about each of the
problems used in the study. Thus, for each student data were gathered on
his method of attacking a number of problems. Also, for each problem data
are available on the methods of attack used by a number of students.

Limitations of the study
Since the primary emphasis in the study was on student variation in
problem-solving, any attempt to characterize problems from these data is
subject to several limitations. The major limitations arise from the sample
of problems and the sample of students involved. In addition, the nature of
the techniques employed in this problem-solving study restricts the types of
data available.

The first limitation is imposed by the restricted range of problems used.
The problems were recognition types of questions selected from examinations
given in the College of the University of Chicago. Although they include questions from each subject field, no attempt was made to select a representative
sample of the types of problems which are available in each field. In addition,
problems requiring more than about five minutes to solve were not used because of limitations of time in securing the data. Another limitation on the
use of more extended problems was the fact that they would have introduced
too many elements of complexity in the task of securing a record of the problem-solving characteristics. These restrictions on the sample of problems
included limit the scope of the study and the kinds of generalizations which
can be drawn from the data.

Another limitation arises from the small number of students for whom
data are available on each problem and from the fact that the sample of students may vary from problem to problem. In general, each problem was giv-
en to at least eight students. These students ranged in age from fifteen to
twenty-five and were at the fiftieth percentile or above on the national norms
for college Freshmen on the American Council on Education Psychological
Examination. The students differed in the length of time they had been in the
College; most had been enrolled for one year. In addition, the level of their
academic achievement differed considerably. Since no attempt was made to
insure that representative samples of students were given each problem, it
is possible that some of the differences between the problems discussed here
may be traced, in part, to variations in the sample of students involved.

The nature of techniques used in collecting the data imposes another
limitation on the results. Students differed in their skill in reporting what

they did as they attacked the problems. In each case, the interviewer attempted to record whatever the student could report as he attacked the problem and supplemented this by questioning the student on points which were not clear. In spite of the precautions, some of the records were so fragmentary that it was necessary to discard them for the purposes of this analysis. While this may have introduced some bias in the sampling of students for each problem, there does not appear to be any clear relationship between the completeness of the problem-solving report and the effectiveness of the problem-solving.

In spite of these limitations, the data on many of the problems are so consistent as to furnish rather clear-cut evidence for a number of generalizations. These generalizations, which could not be clearly derived from data on the products of thought (the solutions chosen), are of value in indicating some of the possible outcomes of this type of investigation. However, the limitations briefly mentioned above do restrict this to an exploratory, rather than definitive, study of problem-solving characteristics.

Classification of problems

In attempting to draw generalizations from the records of what the students said and did when solving the various problems, it was found necessary to classify and analyze the data in a number of different ways. It seemed desirable to relate the schemes of classification and analysis to some of the possible uses of the results.

The first method of classification chosen was to arrange the problems in order of difficulty and to determine the characteristics of each group of problems having the same difficulty level. On this basis, one might expect problems which were solved correctly by 90 per cent of the students to possess characteristics quite different from those answered correctly by 50 per cent of the students, and so on. An analysis of problems failed by a similar proportion of the students did not yield generalizations which would hold for any difficulty level. Although this system did not appear to be a useful and consistent method for organizing the data, it was apparent that evidence on problem-solving characteristics could be a valuable supplement to the item-analysis data on test problems. Such evidence could be especially useful in revealing the sources of difficulty on particular problems.

Another method of classification which was briefly explored was to arrange the problems by subject fields and to determine the characteristics of each group of problems within a subject field. Since the problems selected do not constitute representative samples of the types of problems possible in each subject field, it is not possible to make valid generalizations about an entire subject field or about the difference between subject fields. However, a cursory survey of the data on hand appears to reveal very similar problem-solving characteristics for problems from different subject fields.

Another method of classification which was examined was to arrange the problems by objective-test forms. This involves a comparison of true-false test forms with multiple-choice and master-list forms, etc. Although distinct problem-solving characteristics were not clearly evidenced by test forms, a few of the forms did present specific difficulties for the students. The difficulties revealed by the problem-solving investigation are discussed later in this chapter.

A somewhat more useful scheme for organizing the data was suggested

by similarities in problem-solving records on different problems. It was
noticed that certain types of difficulties on a specific problem were evidenced by one student after another. A close examination of these problems
made the cause of these difficulties apparent. In addition, it was noted that
many students used a similar method of attack on a specific problem. To
a large extent, the method of attack appeared to be dictated by the nature
and form of the problem. This classification of problems by some of the
major types of difficulty they present and by the characteristic method of
attack employed represents a mode of analysis which should be of considerable value to the test constructor. Given an analysis of test problems in
this way, the tester should be able to predict the mental manipulations required for a correct solution. In addition, the tester can determine whether
the difficulties presented by the problem are legitimate difficulties the student should be expected to overcome or whether the difficulties are irrelevant and extraneous to the real problem.

In some ways this classification is closely related to the classification
scheme used in analyzing the problem-solving characteristics of individual
students in chapter ii. One major category in the analysis of problem-solving
characteristics was the student's "Understanding of the Nature of the Problem." This category refers primarily to the student's understanding of the
directions and the specific requirements of the problem. Some of the reasons for this lack of understanding are inherent in the way in which the problem is presented, and these reasons are discussed in the following section
on "Types of Difficulties." Another major category in the analysis of problem-
solving characteristics was the student's "General Approach to the Solution
of Problems," which was further subdivided into the extent of thought about
the problem and the ability to carry through on a process of reasoning. A
few of the characteristic methods of attack as related to these categories
are presented in the section on "Methods of Attack."

Types of difficulties

Each student exhibited a characteristic pattern in his method of attacking problems. The difficulties he had in problem-solving were exhibited in
a great many problems which, superficially at least, appeared to be of very
different kinds. However, certain problems presented specific types of difficulties to many of the students. That is, there appeared to be something in
the nature or the organization of the problem which was a source of difficulty for a large proportion of the students.

An analysis of the problems which proved to be difficult or confusing
to students reveals four major kinds of difficulty. These sources of difficulty may be traced to the format of the problem, the methods by which the
solutions are to be indicated, the use of directions involving negative characteristics, and the use of relative and qualitative terms.

Effect of peculiarities in the format of a test problem. — Occasionally
the form in which a test problem is presented confuses and misleads students. This confusion may be such as to lead some students to attempt to
solve a meaningless problem for which no answer can logically be developed. In other cases, the peculiar format of the problem makes the problem much more complex and difficult than would otherwise be the case.

One source of this difficulty may result from a printing arrangement
in which the alternative answers become confused with the symbols used to

identify the alternatives for marking or recording purposes. This type of difficulty is clearly demonstrated in one problem (see Figure 8) dealing with mathematical symbols.

DIRECTIONS: In each of the following items, select the correct alternative and <u>blacken</u> the corresponding answer space. There may be <u>more than one</u> correct alternative in some items, so be sure to <u>blacken each</u> correct answer space.

$$A- \quad x = 3y$$

$$B- \quad x = y^3$$

$$C- \quad xy = 3$$

$$D- \quad x + y = 3$$

$$E- \quad \frac{x}{2} = \frac{y}{3}$$

112. The equations above in which x is directly proportional to y are (A, B, C, D, E).

113. The equation in which x is inversely proportional to y is (A, B, C, D, E).

Figure 8

Some of the students read the alternatives as "A minus x equals 3y," "B minus x equals y^3," etc. This, of course, made a problem which was impossible to solve. Frequently the student would recognize and correct his error after he attempted to solve the problem and found that it made no sense. This correction usually involved a re-reading of the alternatives accompanied by a sudden reorganization of the material.

Another source of this type of difficulty arises from the use of diagrams or illustrations which are poorly set up, inadequately labeled, or not clearly differentiated from the statement of the problem. One problem included in this investigation was intended to contain two diagrams representing two different stages in a process. The arrangement of the two diagrams, however, led some of the students to see only a single, meaningless illustration. Still another diagram, intended to represent an eclipse of the moon, represented the moon and the earth in an impossible relationship. Since the diagram was presented as correct, many of the students were baffled by the impossibility of reconciling their knowledge of the true relation of the earth and moon with that presented.

A problem which was made more complex by the arrangement of material was one containing a table of data showing height measurements on samples of four different strains of a plant. The figures were arranged in such a way that many of the students saw the data arranged in rows, whereas an interpretation was possible only if the student saw the data as primarily arranged in columns. The discovery of the columnar arrangement of data required much effort on the part of these students, and some students were unable to see the data in the proper form unless this was specifically pointed out.

In many of these problems, the error in the arrangement of the material or the confusing format represented a relatively minor deviation from a correct version. A student given the problem and asked to detect the error would have little trouble in identifying the difficulty and correcting it. However, in an examination the student is under a great deal of pressure. He lacks confidence in his ability to solve the problems and is likely to feel that it is his own fault if a problem is not entirely clear. In addition, he tends to regard the test constructors as authorities on the subject and the test as representing an authoritative version in which everything has a purpose. The student's feeling of insecurity and his acceptance of the test as correct and authentic make it difficult for him to recognize and correct errors or inadequacies in the form and arrangement of the problem material.

The detection of this type of difficulty before the test is given to students is primarily the result of good proofreading and sensitivity to the necessity of proper arrangement of material. However, data on the products of thought, such as statistics on the answers selected by a group, do not reveal the difficulties that errors in problem material present. These difficulties are apparent only if the test constructor is able to simulate the mental processes of a variety of students or if he is able to secure data on the problem-solving characteristics of a group of students on the particular problems involved.

Confusion caused by the method of indicating solutions. — The use of the so-called "objective" type of question or examination problem requires not only that the student determine the appropriate solution but also that he record his solution in the correct manner. Occasionally the method of recording answers may be so ambiguous or complex as to lead students who have the correct solution in mind to record it incorrectly and thus to be appraised in the same way as a student who did not have the correct solution in mind.

DIRECTIONS: Rank the following life forms in the order of their appearance in the geologic record. Blacken answer space A for the one that appeared first, etc.

    81. Mammals
    82. Sponges
    83. Amphibians
    84. Fishes
    85. Flowering plants

Figure 9

Unless problems in which students are to rank or arrange things in a particular order are accompanied by directions which clearly define the extremes of the arrangement, the student may be in doubt as to what is wanted. The problem in Figure 9 illustrates the difficulty resulting from poorly defined extremes. Students were confused as to whether answer A referred to the oldest or the most recent life form, since the "order of appearance" might refer to the order in which they appeared chronologically or to the order in which they would appear as the geologic record is uncovered.

When students are accustomed to one method of indicating answers, they become quite confused if a very different scheme is introduced. Thus, if students have been using a single scheme of classification as applied to a number of items, they have difficulty when a double scheme of classification is used. A problem of the type is shown in Figure 10. Here the students

---

Drama

DIRECTIONS: The dramas which you have studied in this course are listed below in two groups. Each of the statements which follow is to be judged in terms of the dramas in each group. For each statement an odd and an even numbered item are paired together. In making a judgment about the plays in the group marked odd numbers blacken the <u>odd numbered item</u>. In making a judgment about the plays in the group marked even numbers blacken the <u>even numbered item</u>. Identify each statement by blackening the appropriate answer space according to the following key:

Odd Numbers
    A- if the statement is true of Macbeth;
    B- if the statement is true of The Emperor Jones;
    C- if the statement is true of She Stoops to Conquer;
    D- if the statement is true of none of the above plays.

Even Numbers
    A- if the statement is true of The Taming of the Shrew;
    B- if the statement is true of Boris Godunov;
    C- if the statement is true of The Cherry Orchard;
    D- if the statement is true of none of the above plays.

Figure 10

were uncertain whether each characterization was to be related to one or both groups of plays. Several of the students re-read the directions a number of times and were still confused. Some students were unable to start the problem until aided by the interviewer. Other students made use of a scheme of marking the answers but were not at all confident that they were proceeding correctly.

The students' difficulty with the problems illustrated here are clearly the result of inept wording of directions. That the student would have difficulty in determining what to do with these problems should be quite apparent to a careful reader. Careful analysis of problem-solving is not necessary to detect this type of difficulty.

<u>Effect of directions requiring the student to select answers possessing negative characteristics.</u> — In one series of problems (see Figure 11) the students were given several groups of sentences and were directed to se-

lect the worst sentence in each group. Other negative problems involved such

---

DIRECTIONS: One sentence in each of the following paragraphs has been deliberately spoiled — by mistakes in grammar, by transposing the order of words, by adding unnecessary words or by omitting essential words, by trite expressions and inappropriate figures of speech, by changing tenses, by violations of parallel construction, by vagueness in the reference of pronouns, and the like. Since no sentence in ordinary journalistic writing is perfect, you may dislike more than one sentence in each paragraph, but it should be possible to distinguish deliberately spoiled sentences from sentences which are acceptable by ordinary standards. You are to blacken one answer space for each paragraph corresponding to the worst sentence in that paragraph.

106. A — I am deeply concerned about the bill introduced by Representative Wadsworth and Senator Gurney to establish universal compulsory military training.
  B — I feel it is my duty to challenge the wisdom of this bill, not only because I am a student of social and political questions, but I have made a special study of this particular question for nearly fifty years.
  C — I believe that Congress is interested in the opinion of citizens, and especially in the opinion of those who have been careful students of the problems which come before Congress.

Figure 11

---

questions as those shown in Figure 12.

In each of these problems, some of the students tended to forget the type of answer they were looking for as they worked with the material in the problem. They were frequently confused by being confronted with several true alternatives and apparently had forgotten that they were looking for the false or negative alternative. Many of the students found it necessary to reread the problem several times before they could complete it.

"Which of the following is an incorrect explanation of attempts to obtain colonies?"

"Which one of the following dramatic functions is not performed by Laertes?"

Figure 12

The search for a negative type of answer apparently requires the student to make a readjustment of his mental set. The student appears to be oriented toward the selection of true or positive answers, and he has great difficulty in shifting to a search for negative or wrong answers. This is probably the result of being given only a few negative problems in the midst of a large number of positive problems. Even after the student has the directions in mind, his problem-solving on these negative problems appears to be awkward and unnatural.

Undoubtedly, the negative type of problem requires quite distinct and perhaps valuable problem-solving characteristics. It should be noted, however, that the principal element involved, as revealed in this study, is the reorientation to a new type of direction.

Effect of relative terms in a problem. — When directions include such terms as "frequently," "occasionally," "effectively," "most likely," "some," "increasingly," "considerably," etc., students find it difficult to determine the answer required. Under these conditions, students frequently attempt to determine what the examiner has in mind rather than what is an appropriate answer to a particular question. An illustration of this is the problem shown in Figure 13.

Each of the following items consists of a STATEMENT, followed by three COMMENTS on the statement. You are to judge which one is the best comment. The best comment is the one which shows most understanding of the subject discussed in the statement. Blacken the answer space corresponding to the number of the one best comment.

88. If one means by education the matter of going to school, there is equality of education in America.

  1 — There are some slight exceptions to this statement, but it is essentially true to the facts. School attendance is now compulsory in all the states.
  2 — Differences in quality of schooling provided are important in spite of virtual equality of opportunity to attend school.
  3 — Differences in income between individuals and between communities affect both the length and the kind of schools available to most children.

Figure 13

Students were confused by the phrases "best comment" and "most understanding." Some attempted to find the comment which was most in agreement with the original statement. Others took the answer to be the comment which showed most connection to the statement and had difficulty in determining what type of connection was wanted. Others selected the answer which they believed to be the most true and complete comment irrespective of the statement and took the statement as merely setting the general context rather than as an integral part of the problem. Some selected the comment which "throws the most light on the statement." Thus, what seemed to be a clear problem became a fairly confusing one and a different problem for each student. It should be noted that the students who selected the comment on the basis of truth were most likely to get the answer intended by the examiner. In another problem very similar to this, students attempted to find the answer which contradicted the statement most clearly, while others selected an answer which had something on both sides of the question.

When given the question, "Which one of the following has been generally true of labor unions in the United States?" followed by four alternatives, students spent much time in determining what was meant by the term "generally true"; they seemed to feel that this phrase was the most important part of the problem. In problems of this type, the basic confusion seems to be "how far," "to what extent," or "what level" the examiner or test-writer may have in mind. Thus, what one person might think to be an aspect which is generally true might not be quite so widely accepted by another person. "Generally" might refer to importance or significance, historical duration, or to the extent to which different groups are involved. How much emphasis to give to the words "very" and "most likely" also seems to be a great source of difficulty. In answering these questions, the students apparently attempt to get into the frame of mind which they believe the test-writer was in when he formulated the question. They then attempt to estimate the meaning and significance the examiner would attach to these qualitative terms.

It is recognized that qualitative terms such as the ones listed above may be essential as part of many problems. These terms, however, produce a specific set toward the problem and determine, to a large extent, the manner in which the student will proceed to attack it. The examiner, in constructing test problems involving such words, must recognize the effect of these words on the student's method of attack and the kinds of answers which seem appropriate to the student. Such words frequently lead a student to give primary emphasis to the determination of a possible meaning for the term and only secondary attention to the remainder of the problem.

Comments. — When a student is given a problem, it is generally assumed that the recall or recognition of the important ideas in the problem or the manipulation of the problem elements presented are the principal sources of difficulty. It is further assumed that a wrong answer is indicative of the student's failure to employ the correct ideas or to engage in the appropriate mental processes. The types of difficulties presented above indicate that this may not always be the case. In some problems such external considerations as the format of the problem material, the method of recording answers, or the orientation of the student to one type of problem rather than another becomes as important as the problem per se. If a student is able to get the correct answer, it is clear that he has been able to overcome these difficulties and that he is able to employ the correct mental processes or to recognize the correct formulation of an idea. However, if the student gets a wrong answer, it is not clear whether --

1. He is unable to do the correct mental manipulations or to remember the appropriate information, or

2. He is unable to overcome the difficulties of the form in which the problem is set, or

3. Both 1 and 2 apply.

Insofar as tests of achievement are concerned, it would seem desirable to eliminate as many extraneous considerations as possible and to make certain that each problem is really a test of the student's knowledge or of his ability to engage in appropriate mental manipulations. The test-maker can do much to insure this if he is able to simulate the problem-solving activities of the typical students who are expected to take the test. This will be difficult, since the test-maker has lost the essential freshness of viewpoint, both as a result of his superior knowledge of the ideas contained in the problem and as a result of his acquaintance with the problem gained while constructing it. It is probable that he can, to some extent regain this freshness of viewpoint by laying the problem aside for a period of time.

Probably the most direct method of securing evidence on the nature of the problem and the extraneous difficulties it presents is to have a small but carefully selected sample of students attempt to solve it while the test-maker observes. If students are given a relatively brief period of training in "thinking aloud" and are then asked to solve the problem aloud, the observer should be able to collect relatively complete data on what is required of the student by the problem.

Methods of attack

The ways in which students proceed to attack problems throw a great deal of light on the essential nature of the problem. An analysis of the difficulties students encounter on problems is of value in revealing whether the problem is a test of the student's ability to read the directions, his ability to overcome extraneous handicaps, or his ability to perform the essential problem-solving operations. An analysis of the methods used by students in attacking a problem is of value in revealing the mental manipulations required in the problem, the special difficulties of individual students, the presence of extraneous clues to the solution of the problem, and the extent to which the problem is really a test of the knowledge, abilities, and skills intended.

In this exploratory study the ways in which students translated the material in a problem into a more workable form, their reduction of the problem material, and the extent to which they solved a recognition form of test question independent of the alternative answers given by the examiner appeared to be of sufficient importance to warrant a somewhat detailed analysis of the processes involved.

Translation of the ideas and terms of the problem as a step in the attack. -- In attacking many problems, students seem unable to take the material in the form given and solve the problem on that basis. Frequently they change and alter the material in the problem before they do much with it. The extent to which students find it necessary to alter the problem before attacking it appears to be related to the complexity of the problem. On very easy or simple problems the students are apparently able to work with the material as given, and the problem is meaningful in the form presented. In contrast, the more difficult and complex problems require a great deal of alteration before the student is really ready to solve them. On the more complex questions the students appear to substitute one or more questions or subquestions for the given question. In effect, the student cannot communicate with the test constructor until he has altered the material presented in the test problem. In many ways this translation of the test problem into another form is analogous to the defining of terms and rewording of questions which appear to be so necessary if the participants in a serious discussion or argument are to have a "meeting of the minds."

One type of translation involved a change from dates or numbers into words. Figures as such apparently have little meaning for students, and it is only after they have made the figures somewhat more meaningful by substituting appropriate or associated words and phrases that they are able to answer questions involving numbers. Probably one of the clearest examples of this form of translation was in connection with the problem shown in Figure 14.

DIRECTIONS: Each of the following items is an event. Decide in which Period each event occurred. For each item, blacken

answer space 1 if the event occurred in the period 1501—1775 A.D.
answer space 2 if the event occurred in the period 1776—1815 A.D.
answer space 3 if the event occurred in the period 1816—1865 A.D.
answer space 4 if the event occurred in the period 1866—1890 A.D.
answer space 5 if the event occurred in the period 1891—1930 A.D.

11. French and Indian Wars

12. main period of immigration from southern Europe

13. the Spanish-American War

Figure 14

Most students were unable to deal with these dates as given. Evidently, numbers such as 1501, 1861, and 1891 carry little significance until the individual makes certain mental translations or substitutions. In this problem, most of the students found it necessary to substitute the words "Revolution-

---

DIRECTIONS: Each of the following items is a statement about a President of the United States. Select the President to whom the statement best applies. For each item, blacken

answer space 1 if the statement best applies to Jefferson;
answer space 2 if the statement best applies to Jackson;
answer space 3 if the statement best applies to Lincoln;
answer space 4 if the statement best applies to Theodore Roosevelt;
answer space 5 if the statement best applies to Woodrow Wilson.

22. strongly advocated democracy, but emphasized that it would function best in a predominantly agrarian society

23. was the first (of those named in the list) who had to deal with the problems presented by large industrial corporations

24. the prevalence of the spoils system in the federal government is commonly traced back to his administration and to his statement that the duties of public office were so simple that any man could fulfil them.

Figure 15

ary War" for 1776, and to substitue "Civil War" for 1865. The problem then became one of determining whether an event occurred before the Revolutionary War, between the Revolutionary War and the Civil War, after the Civil War, etc. The last period became "recently," or the period before the "New

Deal." Once this translation was made, the task of answering the specific items became fairly simple. A few students who attempted to attack this problem without this type of translation became rather confused. They seemed to devote most of their time to trying to remember the exact date for each item and to determining where that date fitted in with the dates given.

Another type of translation involved a change from proper names to characterizations. Names of individuals have meaning only as the student is able to relate certain events and characteristics to them. Although the questions relating to the names in the problem shown in Figure 15 did supply such characterizations, most of the students appeared to find it necessary to make their own characterizations before proceeding.

The students usually found it to be a more workable problem when they translated the name of the president into a phrase with which they could deal more easily. Thus, one student translated Wilson into "idealist," Jefferson into "man of the people," Roosevelt into "big stick," Lincoln into "Civil War." Another variation on this was Roosevelt into "Rough Riders" and "antitrust," while Wilson became "World War" or "League of Nations." One student found it easier to work with the name Jackson after she had translated it into "unusual inaugural."

A third type of translation was one in which the students took relatively abstract terms or phrases and substituted for them illustrations or more concrete terms and phrases. This type of problem is given in Figure 16.

DIRECTIONS: Without considering the truth or falsity of each of the following statements, blacken answer space

 A- if it is a statement of direct observation;
 B- if it is a theoretical statement based on observation;
 C- if the statement is true by virtue of the definition of
   a quantity contained in the statement.

196. Water freezes at 0°C.

197. The distance from the earth to the sun does not remain
   constant during the year.

199. Air is a mixture.

Figure 16

Here students frequently translated the phrases "direct observation" and "theoretical statement based on observation" into other terms. Thus, some students translated "direct observation" into something that "can be seen, can be weighed, or can be felt." They translated "theoretical" into something that cannot be seen, something that is not observable, and occasionally into something that is vague or must be guessed at. Once a translation of this type had been made, the student was apparently able to deal with a problem with some facility although not necessarily with accuracy.

Sometimes the translation was one which concretized or illustrated some of the terms in the problem. A problem of this kind is shown in

Figure 17. In this problem, most students seemed unable to deal with abstractions such as "country A" and "country B" or to deal with an abstraction of "biological stock" in that form. Some students substituted "United States" and "England" for the countries or "white" and "Negro" for the biological stock. In this problem the substitutions were apparently attempts to support a generalization they had in mind.

In each of the following items you are given an observation recorded by a social scientist, followed by a conclusion based on this observation. Blacken

    answer space 1- if the observation is strong evidence to support the conclusion;

    answer space 2- if the observation is strong evidence to disprove the conclusion;

    answer space 3- if neither 1 nor 2 clearly applies.

66. Observation: The people of country A and of country B speak the same language.

    Conclusion: The people of country A and of country B are descendants from the same biological stock.

68. Observation: In country G scientific knowledge is highly developed.

    Conclusion: There are some cities in country G.

Figure 17

    Still another type of translation differing considerably from the above was one in which the student translated the problem from one type to another. Although this did involve a substitution of one idea for another, or one relationship for another, it appeared to be somewhat more fundamental than the three other types of translation. It was more fundamental in that it appeared to change the entire character of the problem. Thus, in the problem given in Figure 18, the students translated choice A into "relative motion between the magnet and the coil," while choice B became "no relative motion" or "cutting lines of force." Once the student had made this translation, he found it a relatively simple matter to judge each of the items in terms of whether it involved relative motion or not. This translation involved the substitution of a general principle for a specific classification.

    Again, in the problem shown in Figure 19, some of the students translated the problem from order of appearance in the geologic record to order of complexity or to a sequence of water to land life forms. The student thus equated one scheme or classification system to another more familiar or more workable one.

    In all the forms of translation and the illustrations given, it will be noted that altering the materials in the problem apparently makes it more vivid and real to the student. The student appears to have certain things in his memory and must have some key to relate the problem to his memory.

In effect, he must bridge a gap between his mind and the problem. The actual process of translation requires some effort on the part of the student and appears to help him become more actively concerned with the problem at hand.

The diagrams illustrate a magnet M and a coil S on the left and a coil P with battery and switch K and another coil S on the right. The two sets of apparatus (a) and (b) are sufficiently far apart not to influence each other.

The following operations are performed. For each operation, blacken answer space

     A- if a current is induced;
     B- if no current is induced;
     C- if the information given is not sufficient to
        decide between A and B.

133. The magnet is moved toward the coil in (a).

134. The magnet is moved away from the coil in (a).

135. The magnet and coil are moved together without any relative motion in (a).

136. The switch K in (b) is closed.

137. After switch K in (b) is closed, the coil S is moved.

Figure 18

Rank the following life forms in the order of their appearance in the geologic record. Blacken the answer space A for the one that appeared first, etc.

     81. Mammals
     82. Sponges
     83. Amphibians
     84. Fishes
     85. Flowering plants

Figure 19

It was later found that one of the most effective techniques in the remediation of problem-solving difficulties was that of inducing students to make an effort at some type of translation of the material in the problem. It was frequently found that students who were completely baffled by the problem at first glance were, after being induced to attempt to translate it into a different form, readily able to solve it.

It is unlikely that test-workers will be able to make problems which will involve the same type of translation for everyone who attacks them. Translation involves the reworking and rearrangement of the problem material until it is in a suitable form for the examinee to attack it directly. The test constructor should, however, be aware of the types of translation the majority of students must make on a specific problem. He can then determine whether the kinds of translation required represent important and desirable elements in the problem situation. He can, if he so desires, reword the question to eliminate the need for some kinds of translation or revise it to require others. In addition, it should be possible, eventually, to predict the kinds of translation which will be required from the majority of a specific group of examinees for a particular problem. If this can be done, the examination constructor should have a very powerful tool which will enable him to make test problems calling for the pattern of thinking he wishes to elicit.

Reduction of the material in a problem as a step in the attack. — Somewhat different from translation is the process of reduction. Students apparently find it necessary to reduce and simplify the material in a problem as a preliminary step in the attack. Thus, when a student is presented with a problem involving a variety of units, such as feet, yards, and inches, he proceeds to change all the dimensions to a single unit before attacking the fundamental problem presented. When given a set of colored blocks and directed to arrange them in a designated complex pattern or design, the student's first step is to inspect the design for a recurrent motif. Once the motif has been discovered, the student merely has to duplicate the motif arrangement of blocks the proper number of times.

One method of reduction may be seen in the problem given in Figure 20.

DIRECTIONS: For each of the following statements, blacken

answer space 1 if the statement is true;
answer space 2 if the statement is false.

21. The growth of corporations in size and influence in America in the last half-century has been part of a trend toward increasing competition, individualism, and free enterprise in economic life.

Figure 20

In this problem, competition, individualism, and free enterprise apparently became a single idea and each of the three terms became synonymous with the other two. Here, in effect, the students disregarded all except what they believed to be the essential points or material in the problem.

In some problems the reduction seemed to be a technique for eliminating unfamiliar terms. Thus, when asked to judge the statement, "Larger proportion of the population supporting criminal syndicalism and other antilabor, antiradical legislation," as a rural or an urban characteristic, most of the students did not know what was meant by "criminal syndicalism."

After some concern about the meaning of this phrase, they answered the question in terms of antilabor and antiradical legislation and gave the unknown phrase, "criminal syndicalism," no further consideration. They had reduced the problem to the terms and ideas with which they were familiar.

Sometimes the reduction was designed to reduce the number of problems within a larger problem. Thus, when given the question shown in Figure 21, many of the students started by reducing the problem to one of de-

---

DIRECTIONS: In each of the following groups, rank the five items according to the indicated characteristic by <u>blackening</u> answer space

        A- for the item ranking <u>first</u>;
        B- for the item ranking <u>second</u>;
        C- for the item ranking <u>third</u>;
        D- for the item ranking <u>fourth</u>;
        E- for the item ranking <u>fifth</u> and <u>last</u>.

Rank the following in the order of their velocity. <u>Blacken</u> answer space <u>A</u> for the one that travels <u>fastest</u>, etc.

61. Primary earthquake waves

62. The speed of the planet Mercury in its orbit

63. The speed of the earth in its orbit

64. The speed of blue light in water

65. The speed of red light in water

Figure 21

---

termining the relative velocity of earthquake waves, speed of planets, and speed of light. After making judgments about the relative speed of these three kinds of motion, they made finer judgments within each of the groups. This, in effect, reduced the problem to one of comparing three types of motion and then of comparing two specific cases within each of two categories.

In a number of reading problems, the students were given a reading passage followed by a series of statements, each of which was to be classified under one of the following:
        A- if the author of the passage would agree with the statement;
        B- if the author of the passage would disagree with the statement;
        C- if it is impossible to tell if the author of the passage would agree or disagree.
Some of the students who were most successful in solving this type of problem reduced the entire passage to a key sentence, idea, or illustration and then attempted to determine the relation between this key idea or concept and the specific statements. In each case the reduction of the passage to a key version involved the elimination of some of the material in the passage.

Some students performed the reduction by attempting to assign the name of a writer to the passage (the author of the passage was not indicated in the problem) and then relating this writer to the statements. Others reduced the passage to the one sentence in it which they believed to be the key or topic sentence. Others reduced the passage to a general idea and related this idea to the statements.

In all these instances of reduction, it will be noted that the student tends to simplify the material given or to set it up in a form which is easily held in mind. The reduced version eliminates for the student many of the details in the problem which he regards as not required for the solution. Seemingly, the individual finds it difficult to work with more than a limited number of things and must reduce, clarify, and simplify the material before he can work with it conveniently. The reduction frequently does eliminate many of the fine points and significant details in the problem and results in a somewhat more gross judgment than would otherwise be the case. Students differed considerably in their facility in reducing material while retaining the essential elements needed for a correct solution. However, the more successful problem-solvers appeared to reduce and simplify more than did the other students.

Since the reduction eliminates for the students some of the material in the problem, the major question for the test constructor is whether such material is really essential to the problem. If a student can get the correct answer even though he has eliminated from his consideration many of the details in the problem, it is clear that, at least for that student, these details were not needed. If each student reduces the material in about the same way, then the eliminated material is probably of no value in the problem. This type of analysis should reveal whether each part of the problem serves a distinct purpose. Thus, in the question on rural and urban characteristics, the term "criminal syndicalism" does not function except to present a slight handicap to students since they must give some consideration to it before eliminating it. If most of the students can solve a reading problem by selecting a topic sentence and judging each of the questions in terms of that sentence, it is evident that the remainder of the passage is little more than window dressing or that it does little more than decrease the rate at which the student solves the problem.

The test constructor's task is that of setting problems in such a form that students must engage in the proper range of mental operations in order to get the correct answers. If one of the mental operations desired is the selection and elimination of certain material in the problem, it is necessary to establish whether selection and elimination are, in fact, required for a correct solution. If, however, each word in the problem is to be given careful consideration, again it is necessary to determine whether such consideration is really required for the correct solution. In the above examples of reduction, it is clear that some of the material presented in the problem does little more than slow the progress of the student or give to the problem an appearance of complexity which is not really there.

Effect of the form and difficulty of a problem on the independence of the student's attack. — The so-called "new-type" or recognition form of test question may require the use of mental processes somewhat different from those used in the recall form of test question. In the recall form the student is given a question or problem and usually must write out an answer.

Here the student is expected to produce a solution to the given problem. His only choices are among possible alternatives he may be able to produce for himself. In the recognition form the student is given both the question or problem and several alternative answers. His task is that of selecting what he considers the appropriate solution or solutions. It might be expected that the student would have to examine each of the proffered answers and perhaps weigh each of the alternatives against the others before making a choice. In the following discussion and illustrations it will be seen that this is not always the case and that some types of recognition questions more nearly approximate the mental processes required in the recall test form than do others.

Some of the questions are organized and presented in such a way that it is impossible for the student to see the full problem or the real nature of the question until he has examined all the choices given. Under such conditions, the student is prevented from deciding on a possible solution, or may deliberately refrain from making a judgment as to a possible solution, until he has read the alternatives offered. This type of attack was characteristic of problems in which the student is asked to select a comment about a particular idea or concept. This is illustrated in the problem shown in Figure 22.

Which is the best statement about the doctrine of "States' Rights"?

1 -- It has been employed by leaders of both parties as an argument against particular activities of the Federal government.
2 -- It was the accepted American philosophy until the New Deal.
3 -- It has effectively prevented the Federal government from increasing its power.
4 -- It was abandoned as a result of the Civil War.

Figure 22

Here the students generally read the introductory statement and appeared to fix it in mind without making any judgments as to a possible answer. They then read the choices and made a tentative decision about each. Finally, if more than one choice seemed possible, they compared them to determine which was most appropriate. In some cases, when weighing several of the choices, they referred back to the introductory statement before making the final selection. In problems of this type the variety of comments or answers which are possible is exceedingly large and it would be quite uneconomical for the student to attempt to determine the appropriate answer before looking at the choices. Thus, it is impossible to determine the true nature of the given problem until the choices have been examined.

Other types of questions which were approached in a similar fashion are illustrated by Figures 23 and 24. These questions, also, could be followed by a great variety of possible answers. For these questions, the student does not seem to have a solution in mind until he has examined the alternatives offered. In effect, the student reserves a decision about the real nature of the problem until he has read most of the material given in connection with the problem. However, he does make tentative judgments about the choices as he examines them. These problems seem to call for a type of weighing and comparing of choices with a particular set of criteria the student has in mind. The criteria seem to be built up as the student examines the parts of the problem with the full criteria coming to mind after the student has completed his inspection of the entire problem.

DIRECTIONS: For each of the following items, blacken the answer space corresponding to the letter of the one best answer or completion.

174. Which one of the following was an idea which had considerable influence on American foreign policy between 1920 and 1930?

    A — The best contribution the United States can make toward world peace is to bring about the reduction of armaments.

    B — The United States will obtain great benefits in the long run by supporting a system of collective security.

    C — A system of defensive and offensive alliance with foreign powers is the best guarantee of world peace.

    D — The activities of Latin-American countries are no longer the concern of the United States.

Figure 23

---

177. Which one of the following has been generally true of labor unions in the United States?

    A — They have advocated government ownership and operations of industrial enterprises.

    B — They have advocated the incorporation of all labor groups into one nation-wide union.

    C — They have advocated collective bargaining as a fundamental right of labor.

    D — They have advocated direct representation of labor in Congress.

Figure 24

Another type of question in which students were able to make judgments about the solution only after completing the examination of the problem is shown in Figure 25. It is apparent that these questions are complete without the choices. However, they proved to be very difficult questions, and most of the students were unable to think of the solutions independently. It was only after examining each of the alternatives that they could think of a possible solution. That is, they depended on the choices to suggest possible solutions. Once such possibilities were suggested, they could make a decision to determine which was the most appropriate or correct answer. Here, again, the criteria for a correct answer were built up as the student examined all the parts of the problem.

In contrast to the types of problems discussed above are the problems which students attack by arriving at a type of answer, a hypothesis as to the proper answer, or by setting up criteria the answer must meet, before looking at the alternative choices offered. These problems are set up in such a

---

DIRECTIONS: In the following items, blacken the answer space corresponding to the one best response.

10 Dirty snow melts more quickly than clean snow. This best illustrates the principle that (A- good conductors of heat are good absorbers of heat; B- poor reflectors of light are good absorbers; C- white materials absorb most visible wave-lengths of light; D- irregular surfaces diffuse incident radiation; E- radiation cannot penetrate opaque bodies).

13 Eggs cook more rapidly if boiled in sea water than in fresh water because (A- salt penetrates the shell and hardens the contents; B- sea water boils at a higher temperature; C- sea water has a higher vapor pressure; D- sea water contains minute amounts of catalysts).

Figure 25

way as to stimulate most of the students to attempt to arrive at the nature of the solution before examining the choices. The examination of the choices merely becomes a procedure for finding a choice that fits the pattern the student has in mind. In these problems, the choices play a very minor role in the problem-solving, and the original statement of a problem becomes the important factor. All the problems attacked in this way were such that the introductory statement or question gave a relatively complete statement of the problem.

Figure Analogies

In each line below, find the rule by which Figure A is changed to make Figure B. Apply the rule to Figure C. Select the resulting figure at the right and blacken the corresponding answer space.

Figure 26*

One type of problem characterized by this type of attack is illustrated by Figure 26. Here the student read or examined Figures A and B, set up a tentative rule, then examined Figure C and stated something about the type of answer he was looking for. He then inspected the various choices very

---

*L. L. Thurstone and Thelma Gwinn Thurstone, American Council on Education Psychological Examination for College Freshmen, 1943 edition. Princeton, New Jersey: Cooperative Test Division, Educational Testing Service.

quickly and selected the one which most nearly agreed with the solution he had in mind. In examining the choices offered, the student seemed to give only a fleeting glance to most of the choices and the appropriate choice seemed to "pop out"; that is, the choice which conformed to the solution he had in mind seemed to stand out in strong contrast to the remaining choices. This problem appears to be attacked in this way primarily because of two characteristics. Because it is relatively simple, students had little difficulty in thinking of an appropriate answer. Also, the directions for this problem instruct the student to formulate a rule on the basis of the first pair of figures and to apply it to the third figure. Thus, the directions, in effect, call for a solution before the choices are to be examined.

Another type of problem which students attacked in this manner is illustrated by Figure 27. Here the student read the introductory statements,

---

DIRECTIONS: In each of the following items, you are given statements and four conclusions. Assume that the statements are true. You are to judge which of the conclusions then logically follows; i.e., must be true if the statements are true. Blacken the answer space corresponding to the one conclusion which logically follows. If none of the conclusions logically follows, blacken answer space E.

STATEMENTS:

Any action that impedes the war effort of the United States should be made illegal. All criticism of the government by manufacturers impedes the war effort of the United States.

CONCLUSIONS:

    A. Justifiable criticism should be permitted, but mere faultfinding should be made illegal.
    B. Preservation of the right to criticize is as important as winning the war.
    C. All criticism of the government by manufacturers should be made illegal.
    D. Some criticism of the government by others as well as by manufacturers should be made illegal.
    E. (None of the foregoing conclusions follows.)

Figure 27

stated a conclusion, and then examined the alternative conclusions to determine which one most nearly fitted the solution he had in mind. Although most of the students had the correct solution in mind for this particular problem, they examined each of the choices rather carefully on the possibility that their solution might not be entirely correct. They seemed to be unwilling to depend on the solution they had in mind. The organization of this problem makes it rather natural for the student to think of a solution before examining the choices. The completion of the syllogism follows logically from the major and the minor premises.

Another kind of problem attacked in this way is illustrated by Figures 28 and 29. These are primarily questions of information, and the students

---

The following items deal with the ideas and practices of several social systems. Each item consists of a statement about a social system, and names two systems to which it <u>may</u> apply. For each item blacken the answer space corresponding to the number of the <u>best</u> answer.

158. The theory assumes that human beings are naturally good, but the state is necessarily evil. The system is (1- anarchism 2- liberal democracy 3- both of these systems 4- neither of these systems).

Figure 28

DIRECTIONS: A series of terms to be defined are underlined in the following items. From the alternatives given, choose the definition which you believe to be the <u>best one</u> and <u>blacken</u> the answer space on the answer sheet which corresponds to its letter.

96. <u>Isotopes</u> are (A- molecules having different arrangement of the atoms B- substances having the same percentage composition C- atoms having the same nuclear charge but different atomic weight D- atoms having the same atomic weight but different nuclear charge E- atoms having the same nuclear charge but different arrangement of planetary electrons).

Figure 29

who possessed the necessary information thought of the solution, or the characteristics the solution should contain, before inspecting the choices.

In a number of problems, although the student did have an answer in mind after he had read the question or statement of the problem, he was unwilling to depend fully on his own solution. In these problems, the student set up his solution as one of several possibilities. He then examined the choices to determine the choice which was nearest to the solution he had in mind and to determine whether any of the answers offered had characteristics not included in his solution. This was illustrated in the problem presented in Figure 27, as well as in the problem shown in Figure 30.

In this problem, most of the students thought of the national government as a solution before looking at the choices, but they then seemed quite willing to abandon this solution as they found others which appeared more tempting. This type of approach seemed especially to characterize problems which involve computation. In such problems the student made the necessary computations and had a tentative answer in mind before examining the choices. He then inspected the choices to find the one which was nearest to the answer he had in mind. If none of the choices agreed with the one he had in mind, he attempted to find a new solution. It was noted that, when the test question was in multiple-choice form and one of the choices was "None of the above answers," the student made fewer attempts to re-work the problem when the answer he had in mind differed from the choices offered.

During the last 10 years, as compared with previous periods, the initiative in providing for the economic security of the individual has increasingly been assumed by:

1 -- the individual concerned
2 -- the employer of the individual
3 -- the labor unions
4 -- the Federal government

Figure 30

The recall or free-response test form is intended to evoke an independent solution from the student. If problems of this type are not clearly stated, the student is at a loss to determine exactly what the problem is, and he may respond by structuring it in a way different from that anticipated by the examiner. On the other hand, if the problem is stated too precisely, the student may respond with a stereotype which has some relevance to the problem but which does not involve any real independence of thought. A type of attack which involves the independent production of a solution is most likely to occur when the statement of the problem is complete without the choices, when the problem requires the student to set up a principle and apply it to given material, and when one of the choices permits the student to reject any of the specific answers given and to select an alternative ("None of the above," "Correct answer not given," etc.) which can include any answer he may have in mind.

The objective test forms have not usually been thought to require independent solutions. The objective test forms have frequently been condemned because they appear to require only recognition of appropriate answers and memorized responses. Perhaps a more valid criticism of objective test forms is that the student may select the correct answer on the basis of clues which are irrelevant to the real problem to be attacked.

The major task for the examination constructor is to set up problems which will evoke the appropriate problem-solving behavior from the student if he possesses the competence being measured. In the illustrations and discussions in the preceding sections of this chapter, it is apparent that objective test forms, if they are carefully made, can evoke the appropriate problem-solving behavior.

Methods of attack on a single type of problem

The preceding sections have been devoted to an attempt to draw generalizations about the ways in which students attack selected examination problems. Each generalization applied to problems which varied greatly in form and subject matter. These data demonstrate how problems which superficially appear to be quite different are attacked in a similar fashion.

A somewhat different result is evident when a series of problems which superficially appear to be similar are analyzed to determine the method of attack employed. Here the interviewer was primarily concerned with the

63

techniques by which students decide on the appropriate answer. Several vocabulary-test items were selected because they represented a relatively simple illustration of problems appearing in the same general form. The problems given are shown in Figure 31.

DIRECTIONS: For each of the following words in the column at the left, five alternatives are given. Select for each of the words in the left-hand column the alternative word or phrase which corresponds most closely in meaning. On the answer sheet, blacken the answer space whose number corresponds to the number of the alternative which you have selected. If you are not sure of the correct answer, select one by guessing.

34. anomalous   1- deceitful   2- difficult   3- irregular
                   4- nameless   5- similar

35. bestial   1- dumb   2- superior   3- robust
               4- brutish   5- hideous

45. portent   1- mobile   2- mystic   3- omen
               4- conceited   5- disaster

49. corpulent   1- roguish   2- material   3- portly
                 4- sadistic   5- well-dressed

53. designation   1- appellation   2- assessment
                  3- outline   4- quietude   5- apparition

61. fatuous   1- inflated   2- silly   3- ominous
               4- destined   5- humorous

Figure 31

Data were available on only six to eight students on these test items. In no one of the items did all the students use the same method of attack. However, in each item, two or more of the students used a similar technique for getting an answer. Since they attacked the problems quite independently, it is likely that the techniques are general ones, and it is quite probable that a relatively large portion of other students in similar circumstances would approach the problems in much the same fashion.

A characteristic method of solving the simple vocabulary items may be described as direct association. Here the student takes the problem word and equates it directly with one of the choices. Thus, in problems 35 and 49 the majority of the students had little difficulty in equating bestial with brutish, and corpulent with portly. For these students the other choices seemed to play little part.

A slightly different technique was one in which the students found a synonym for the problem word and then equated one of the choices to this synonym. Thus, in 53, the students said that designation means name, a pointing-out, or a place to go. They then decided that appellation means the same thing.

A third technique was one in which the students analyzed the problem word on the basis of the foreign-language root involved and then found the synonym which most nearly agreed with the root meaning. Thus, in 34, several of the students decided that nom in anomalous referred to name and that a referred to without. These students then selected nameless as the synonym. Although this was a perfectly good method of problem-solving, it did not help these students in finding the correct response — irregular. This technique, however, did aid several of the students in getting the correct synonym for corpulent in 49. Here they related corpus to the Latin for body, then selected portly as the most appropriate term to apply to body. A few students went from body to fat and then to portly.

A technique which was used less frequently with this particular group of words was that based on similarity of parts of speech and other accidental clues. Thus, in item 45, several of the students decided that portent sounded like a noun and that omen was the only other noun which could apply. They ruled out mobile and conceited on the grounds that these were not similar parts of speech.

Other techniques were encountered during the problem-solving investigations which are not illustrated here. With some of the vocabulary-test questions, the students used the problem term in a sentence and then tried the most probable of the choices in the same sentence. When they found a choice which sounded right, they decided it was the correct answer. This was a type of aesthetic judgment rather than one made on the basis of any clearly recognized criteria. Another technique was to make a relatively formal definition of the problem term and then to locate the choice which most nearly satisfied one or more aspects of the definition. In a few cases the student went from the problem term to a series of synonyms, then to the answer choice. That is, a chain of synonyms established the relation between the problem term and the correct choice in the test question.

Data of the kind described above should be very useful to the test constructor in determining how to proceed in the construction of new test items. An investigation of this type, when carried on in greater detail on a larger number of cases, should reveal the kinds of mental processes involved in answering vocabulary-test questions of the form illustrated here. Such mental processes enable the test constructor to determine the value or various alternatives, to select words and choices which will most nearly bring out a particular mental process, as well as serve to indicate one possible classification of test items for diagnostic purposes. Given a careful investigation on a particular test form, it should be possible to make test questions such that each answer or product can be related to a particular mental process.

Summary

The data on test problems based on item analyses, correlations, and other statistical procedures are of value in refining a particular test. These data enable the test-maker to eliminate problems which are ambiguous, which reduce the reliability, or which are not highly correlated with some criterion. Such data should also enable the test-maker to make parallel tests which will have similar statistical properties. Data may also be used to select test items which have similar statistical properties.

Such data do not give the test constructor very much insight into the nature of the mental manipulations the examinee must make and the sources of difficulty in the problem. They do not disclose the extent to which a test exercise represents a similar problem for all who attack it. Data of this type do not reveal the alterations the student makes in the test problem as he attacks it and the variety of solutions he may produce.

The reactions of the student in the context of a test situation would appear to represent the basic kinds of information the test constructor must have if he is to do more than improve the statistical picture of a test. If he is to gauge the value of the problem or the test exercise, he must have insight into the thoughts, feelings, and mental operations of the student when confronted with a specific problem. Until he has such insight, the test constructor can only proceed by trial and error, making many test exercises and retaining those which have appropriate statistical properties.

The data reported in this chapter reveal the kinds of insight which may be gained into the nature of a specific problem by an attempt, however exploratory, to probe the student's reactions and behavior. Such an investigation presents many difficulties, both in securing and in analyzing the data. Such studies, if carried on in sufficient detail and with extreme care, should enable one to predict the effect of each word and phrase in the statement of a problem. The test constructor who makes such investigations should more fully understand his testing techniques and should improve his skill in constructing test problems.

In addition to improving the test worker's skill in constructing problems, these investigations into the nature of the mental processes in a problem situation should enable one to interpret the results of tests more adequately and completely.

CHAPTER IV

REMEDIATION OF PROBLEM-SOLVING

The requirements for the Bachelor's degree in the College of the University of Chicago are stated in terms of comprehensive examinations. The students may take these examinations whenever they believe they are ready to do so. Each of the examinations is six hours in length and includes a great variety of problems peculiar to the particular subject field. The examination questions range from problems requiring little more than the remembering of specific items of information to problems in which the student needs little information but must make use of certain skills and abilities emphasized in the course.

Since each of the examinations contains a great variety of problems, the writers were of the opinion that some of the failures on these comprehensive examinations might, in large measure, be explained on the basis of ineffective problem-solving methods. In an effort to apply some of the findings on the differences in the problem-solving methods of individuals (as discussed in chapter ii), we became concerned about the possibility of changing the problem-solving of selected students in the College.

We recognized that many of the failures on the comprehensive examinations could be attributed to insufficient preparation on the part of the student as well as to low scholastic aptitude. Thus, if a student has a much lower scholastic aptitude than the majority of the other students in the class, he is greatly handicapped by the level at which the ideas in the course are presented, as well as by the rapidity with which new ideas are introduced. If the student has made insufficient preparation for the examination, he will not have mastered the essential information called for in many of the problems. Although, theoretically, such individuals might be aided by problem-solving training, we did not believe their primary source of difficulty was poor problem-solving methods. Also, we did not believe they would exhibit significant changes as the result of a relatively short period of training in problem-solving.

Criteria for selection of the remedial group

In order to select students whose failure on the comprehensive examinations might be due in large part to poor problem-solving methods, a group of students who met certain requirements were invited to participate in an experimental venture in problem-solving remediation. The criteria for admission to the group were:

1. Their scholastic aptitude, as measured by the American Council on Education Psychological Examination, by a reading comprehension test, and by a writing skills test, was relatively higher than their achievement on the comprehensive examinations. This requirement gave some indication that their failure on the comprehensive examinations was probably attribut-

able to factors other than low scholastic aptitude.

2. They had, according to their assertions, devoted at least an average amount of time to study. In interviews some of the students admitted that they had not studied as much as they might have, but still they felt that they had done enough work to enable them to make at least a passing grade. In most cases, after one or more interviews, we also were of the opinion that they had studied enough to master the basic information required on the comprehensive examinations.

3. They claimed that the examination did not adequately reflect their understanding and mastery of the subject. Some of the students said that they were not able to do their best work because of nervousness at the time of the examination. They also complained that they had great difficulty in making use of their knowledge of the subject matter and their understanding of the field when given the problems posed in the examination. That is, they were apparently unable to attack effectively the specific problems included in the comprehensive examinations.

Since we wished to experiment on problem-solving remediation under favorable conditions, we made efforts to insure that the first group of students to be included in the experiment were highly motivated. Most of the students had been put on probation because of failure on the comprehensive examinations, and their remaining in the College was contingent upon their passing one or more comprehensive examinations within a period of three months. In addition, these students were willing to devote at least ten hours of time, over a period of six weeks, to the problem-solving sessions and at least two hours a week to practice on specific aspects of the problem-solving technique.

In order to make it possible to secure evidence of change on the comprehensive examination performance within a period of three months, we selected only students who were planning to repeat one or more comprehensive examinations in September, 1945. All had failed one or more comprehensive examinations in June, 1945.

Problem-solving techniques

In considering methods of remediation, we made the major assumption that the problem-solving characteristics of an individual are the reflections of habits which the individual has developed over a relatively long period of time. Such habits of problem-solving may vary in their effectiveness in producing good or correct solutions to particular problems. These habits determine the ways in which individuals attack the problems they encounter on examinations, in discussions, and in their studying. This assumption appeared to be reasonable in light of the consistency in the problem-solving characteristics exhibited by individuals from problem to problem, as discussed in chapter ii.

We further assumed that the habits of problem-solving, like other habits, could be altered by appropriate training and practice. The first task of the problem-solving remediation, then, became one of analyzing the individual's problem-solving methods and determining the points at which they were inadequate or the ways in which they handicapped him in his attack on problems. The second task in remediation was to determine the necessary measures to remedy these inadequacies.

Review of the literature on improving methods of thought

Although there are many published articles and books on how to improve one's thinking, relatively few have been based on well-controlled observations or experiments. Many of the published reports emphasize a hortatory approach to the problem, and involve logical suppositions rather than experimentally substantiated findings. Several such reports are referred to below as illustrations of the kind of study and generalizations usually made.

Parker (16), in his discussion of practice in thinking, lists some rules for training pupils in effective problem-solving. These rules, intended for use by teachers, include defining the problem; keeping it clearly in mind; stimulating suggestion through analysis and recall; evaluating suggestions through open-mindedness, criticism, and verification; and keeping the discussion organized through the use of such auxiliaries as graphs, summaries, and outlines. The basis for these rules is not given. Presumably, they were derived from the writer's experiences.

Polya's analysis (18) presents a method for solving problems efficiently, based on an examination of mathematical problems. His rules for attacking a problem are:

"First, you have to understand the problem. . . .Second, find the connection between the data and the unknown. You may be obliged to consider auxiliary problems if an immediate connection cannot be found. You should obtain eventually a plan of solution. . . .Third, carry out your plan. . . .Fourth, examine the solution obtained."

In Polya's discussion, much depends on the luck of the problem-solver in coming forth with "bright ideas." Little is said as to just how these "good guesses" are produced. He is apparently describing what should happen in the solution of a problem rather than what actually takes place.

Another approach to improvement of one's thinking is an experimental one, in which the experimenters have tried to secure evidence on specific aspects of problem-solving remediation. Several of these studies are reported below.

Lapp (9) has demonstrated that practice in solving physics problems increases achievement in physics. It would follow that practice in problem-solving is necessary, but in the study as reported, Lapp gives no indication of what accompanied the practice. It is difficult to imagine how practice without further instruction would be beneficial if the subjects were attacking problems incorrectly and repeatedly used those incorrect methods.

In another experimental approach, MacLatchy (11) investigated the difficulties children have in solving arithmetic problems. She found that these difficulties arise from the seeming invariability of the methods of solving problems, with overemphasis on the following of a pattern. She demonstrated that this could be overcome by having the children solve a problem in as many different ways as possible.

MacLatchy's finding would seem to be substantiated by Maier's experiment on set in problem-solving (12). Maier conducted an experiment to determine the effect of habitual direction on the solution of a problem. He found that good reasoners do not indefinitely pursue unsuccessful attacks on a problem but that poor reasoners do. He is of the opinion that reasoning is, at least in part, the process of overcoming such habitual responses. He also believes that, although one cannot endow a person with the very best equipment necessary for the solution of problems, persons can be trained to attack the problem so that the solution is not prevented from appearing. When the subjects were given hints on how to reason (such as directions to seek an entirely different method of solution if the attempted method failed and to keep an open mind for new meanings in old situations), there was an increase in correct solutions to the given problems. Maier also found that both good and poor reasoners profited by these suggestions. This would seem to support the findings in the remedial study reported by the writers.

Hildreth (6) did an experimental study of puzzle-solving with jigsaw puzzles, in which some of the subjects did, and others did not, have a picture of the completed puzzle before beginning the solution. The experimenter found that the subjects worked better if they saw the complete picture beforehand — the "with understanding" situation. Working without any clues at all was much more difficult. Hildreth concluded: "School problem-solving will be more successful to the extent that the pupils can be given an overview of the whole, some knowledge of the central meaning of the problem, some meaningful clues to aid solution."

O'Neill (15), in a study similar to the remedial program described by the present writers, conducted a clinic to train students in the fundamentals of thinking by providing drill in thinking through problems. The students in the clinic would solve the problems in the group and then discuss their answers, trying to discover where their reasoning was not adequate. The experimenter found that the thought-process cannot be divorced from technical information. A check on the grades of the students after attendance at the clinic showed improvement.

In an attempt to effect remediation in arithmetic with school children, Buswell and John (3) devised a diagnostic test in which the student "thinks aloud" as he solves problems. His errors and deviations are then analyzed and can be corrected. This study was of special interest to the writers because of the method used to secure evidence on problem-solving processes.

These studies have taken several different approaches to the problem of remediation, with varying degrees of success. All, however, appear to be optimistic about the possibilities of improving the individual student's ability to solve problems. Although the remedial study reported in the following section started with somewhat different problems and assumptions, the findings of the study are in harmony with those of the experimental studies mentioned here.

Study of remedial group in problem-solving

After a consideration of the literature, we were of the opinion that the most fruitful approach was likely to be an empirical one, based on college students and examination problems used in the College program. We were willing to make the assumption that the students who most consistently perform at the A grade-level on the comprehensive examinations are likely to possess the most effective problem-solving characteristics. It is possible to secure such high grades as a result of an inordinate amount of study, interest in the subject field, and unusually high scholastic aptitude. However, to get such grades consistently, the individual must, in all probability, also have good problem-solving methods. For our purposes the records on the problem-solving of these extremely successful students (as reported in chapter ii) appeared to offer the most useful source of evidence on what constitutes good problem-solving methods.

With this assumption granted, the task of determining the individual student's weaknesses in problem-solving became one of discovering the consistent differences in problem-solving between the failing student and the highly successful student. Such differences could, of course, be seen most quickly if both groups of students attacked the same problems under as nearly the same conditions as possible.

A small number of problems were selected from those used in the study on the problem-solving characteristics of successful and nonsuccessful students. These problems were used because they exhibited the following characteristics:

1. No great amount of specific and technical information was necessary for their solution. We were interested in improving the student's problem-solving habits rather than the extent of his information or knowledge in each of the subject fields. Also, questions of information are not very fruitful in revealing the individual's problem-solving characteristics.

2. They were illustrative of the kinds of problems and test forms the student would encounter in examinations for the different courses. It was felt that such problems would be regarded as important by the students, since they could easily see the relationship between the comprehensive examinations and work on these problems.

3. They were the problems which appeared to reveal most clearly differences between the methods of attack used by successful and nonsuccessful problem-solvers. Such problems were regarded as most likely to reveal the nature of the individual student's difficulties in the limited amount of time available for interviewing each student.

Securing the record on the individual student

Each of the students was given a brief statement about the nature of problem-solving and our ideas about its remediation. This statement was intended to prepare the students for the later analysis sessions, when we desired to have them look at the results as objectively as possible, and also to remove some of the mystery from the procedures.

The students were told that very little is known about the nature of the mental processes involved when a person attacks problems. However, one helpful way of thinking about it is to analogize it to a physical activity, such as tennis or golf. It was pointed out that the individual's mode or habit of thinking has developed over a period of time and is the result of a great variety of experiences and circumstances. At present, the individual is probably not very conscious of what he does when he solves problems. In the same way, the methods and movements a person uses in playing tennis or golf are the result of a variety of experiences and circumstances, and the individual plays the game without being very conscious of what he is doing or how he is doing it at a particular moment.

The statement informed the students that in the problem-solving sessions an attempt would be made to find out what each student does as he attacks various problems selected from the examinations given in the College. After these records had been secured, an effort would be made to make the student conscious of what he does in solving problems. These problem-solving methods would then be compared with the methods used by consistently successful students in the College. The student should look upon this comparison in much the same way as he would if he were to compare his methods of playing tennis with the methods used by a champion tennis-player. It was emphasized that the expert might do some very awkward things, and some of the steps in his playing might not really be any better than those used by the novice. However, any comparison of the novice and the champion would attempt to disclose those differences which made the game of the champion more effective.

Aside from the differences in technique between the champion and the novice, there might also be differences in confidence. The more success-ful tennis-player might play a better game largely because he was confi-dent of his ability. Thus, it was pointed out, it would be difficult and per-haps impossible to return a tennis ball at the far end of the court if one did not make a great effort and if one did not have some confidence in the pos-sibility of making the return shot. This applies equally well to problem-solving, where great mental effort might be required to attack a particular problem. Unless one made this effort and had some assurance of possible success, there would be little likelihood of successfully solving the problem.

It was further pointed out that knowing what to do was not sufficient. Thus, in tennis one might know all the proper things to do but never actually do them. Knowledge of a skill must be accompanied by a sufficient practice to develop facility in its use. In problem-solving, the student must not only determine what are the desirable methods but must actually practice the use of these methods until they become habits. If the methods were not prac-ticed sufficiently, they might even become harmful to the student, in the same way that an attempt to make a change in one's tennis-playing before a big match would probably lead to disaster unless the individual developed the techniques to a point where he did not have to think consciously about them before using them.

It was emphasized that remediation in problem-solving was not the same as learning tricks of taking an examination. We were attempting to develop desirable methods of problem-solving which would apply to all types of problems. It was further pointed out that many of the examination problems required knowledge of specific technical terminology, principles, and concepts found in the appropriate subject fields. No attempt would be made to provide this knowledge in the problem-solving sessions; the student would have to se-cure such knowledge entirely on his own.

Finally, it was pointed out that this work was largely experimental and that little could be promised the student in the way of improvement. He was told that there seemed to be some promising leads which, however, might not necessarily work for him or for the others involved in the initial exper-iment.

After this fairly extensive preparation, the student was given some sim-ple mathematical problems and asked to tell how he solved each. He was giv-en about fifteen minutes of training in "thinking aloud" as he solved these simple problems. He was then given some of the selected problems, and records as complete as possible were made of his problem-solving. If the record made as the student attacked the problem did not appear to be re-vealing, he was questioned on his method after he had completed the prob-lem. A few of the students had great difficulty in verbalizing their methods of problem-solving, and the interviewer had to be content with getting what-ever evidence these students could give after they had completed the prob-lem.

From time to time the students were questioned about any differences between their ways of attacking problems in the interview situation and their methods in an actual examination situation. On the whole, the students felt that their reports in the experimental situation were not a great deal different from those which might be obtained under real examination conditions, except for a feeling of being slowed down because of the verbalizing, or "thinking aloud," aspect of the situation. Two sessions of one and one-half hours each were devoted to recording the student's method of attack on the selected problems.

At the third session the analysis of the student's methods was begun. The solution he had given to a particular problem was reviewed, and then the solution of the successful problem-solver, or "model" student, was read. The remedial student was asked to find and list any differences in method between the two solutions, disregarding the accuracy of either answer. (The "model" solution was a solution chosen from the records of the A students in which the methods used were most easily and clearly differentiated from those used by the nonsuccessful students.) Usually, for the first few examples, the student could not see just what was meant by a difference in method, and he was pretty much on the defensive, saying, "I don't really see any difference," or "We both seem to have done it much the same way," and so on. The interviewer would then try to point out the differences and, if they existed, the similarities in method between the model and the remedial student's attack. The interviewer emphasized that the student was to observe the differences in method without making judgments about the value of these differences.

The students listed these differences in their own words. It was suggested that a difference between the model and the remedial student which recurred many times in many types of problems was probably a source of difficulty for the remedial student and would be worthy of further attention. It was also suggested that a difference which was noticed once, or only a few times, might be merely an artifact of the problem and not serious. The students were, therefore, to look for consistency of difference between their methods and those of the model student.

The writers felt that it was important for the student himself to find the differences in method. One reason for this was the abstract character of these differences in method; we believed that, if the student found the difference himself, we could be a little more sure that he comprehended it than if it had been pointed out to him by the interviewer. Another reason for this procedure was the increased likelihood that the student would accept the differences in method if he could discover them himself. Some of the emotions aroused by the remedial students' sense of failure and inadequacy and their antagonism toward the interviewer appeared to be somewhat tempered by their search for, and discovery of, the differences. This technique of discovery helped the students to see the importance of the differences in the attack on problems, especially when the same difficulty was found repeatedly.

Three samples of the original lists of differences between the student and the model are given below. The students were instructed to make a list of the differences for their own use and were later asked to make a copy for the interviewer. Some of the variations in the lists of problem-solving differences are interesting to note.

One of the outstanding characteristics of the list made by Jean is its subjective quality, with the differences listed in terms of "he" and "I." Again, these differences are stated in terms of difficulties with specific problems rather than in general terms which might pertain to any problem. There is, however, a change in attitude evidenced as she compiled the list, starting with a very subjective statement, "I didn't think it necessary to formulate the general rule," and ending with a somewhat more objective observation on the method, with little in the way of value judgment. There is an air of defiance in the repeated, "Got it right, though," despite the fact that the instructions were to ignore the accuracy of the response.

Jean's List

1. I didn't think it necessary to formulate the general rule.
   Generalization too broad.
   Verbalization reversed actually.
2. Lack of understanding of given terms.
   Define and illustrate as alternatives.
   I looked for "true" and "false" — others looked for "best." Didn't interpret directions properly.
   I looked for answer — didn't have an answer before I looked. Higher degree of inaccuracy. (I get this O.K. with syllogisms.)
3. He associated and brought in intermediary event with dates. I did the same with the second part, but didn't know country.
4. He employed an illustration for proof.
   Should set up criteria for an answer; if not enough, set up illustrations and examples.
5. Didn't get essential terms of what I was looking for before I began reading alternatives.
   Jumped to conclusion without carrying illustrative reasoning through.
   Did read terms thoroughly but didn't keep them in mind; reversed them.
6. Didn't define terms of statements. Got it right through outside example.
7. Should pull out main words. Got it right, though.
8. Didn't establish relations between terms. Got it right, though.
   Careless about selecting right alternative.
   Keeping directions in mind. I think in terms of "true" and "false" instead of "scientific study," etc.

Contrasting Jean's list with that of Ralph's below, we see a shift in emphasis from the specific to the general formulation of differences. Ralph's differences or "rules" might be applied to any problem. (It should be noted that this is not the original list of differences formulated in the interview situation, but rather an edited copy of what the student inferred from these differences.) Where Jean's list places greatest emphasis on directions and terminology, Ralph's involves a greater variety of difficulties.

Ralph's List

1. Find rule or formula that applies to problem under consideration.
2. Apply rule and formulate answer, then check with offered answers.
3. Progress into problem by formula which has been generalized

through application.
4. Rules should deal with specific problem.
5. Try to read directions clearly the first time.
6. Do not answer by guessing or supposition.
7. Think before the formulation of answer.
8. Direct thought in stream which has been pointed in the direction of the problem at hand.
9. Emphasis on the major ideas in the problem, not all ideas.
10. Box off ideas into main question in the problem.
11. Reason from known knowledge or examples.
12. In graphs formulate a specific picture.

Tom's list displays a rather high level of generalization in the formulation of the differences. It is quite apparent that the areas in which he experienced difficulty are different from those of Ralph. Tom's problem-solving methods were inconsistent and his general approach haphazard, while Ralph's chief difficulty was his inability to focus on the problem at hand.

Tom's List

Differences of approach to questions between model student and Tom

1. Directions comprehended on first reading by model, but not by Tom. Even after comprehending questions, Tom does not adhere to them.
2. In a series of relationships having general differences, the whole series is not examined by Tom, and they are by the model. (In a word, the problem was not read through.)
3. Tom continually refers to prior problems, causing confusion with immediate problem.
4. Model forms generalities giving general rules, making all problems (of a particular type) clearer, Tom gives particular name for each part of each different problem.
5. Skipping problems by Tom advantageous?
6. Model anticipates answer and then looks for it. Tom checks possible answers first, by the long and fallible process of elimination.
7. In the master-list question, model types or generalizes possible answers first. Tom reads individual questions first and then goes back to all the possible answers.
8. Again in master-type question, model finds basis and then criteria for answer in previous subject matter, then finds appropriate answer to current question; but not Tom.
9. Model uses all possible information and clues to find the answer. Does Tom?
10. Model reduces idea of statements to key terms, finds relationship of these terms, and judges accordingly (with respect to the question at hand).
11. When handling objective questions, refrain from subjective reasoning.

It is evident from these lists that this method of analysis reveals variations in the problem-solving difficulties recognized by different students, variations in the willingness of the students to accept these difficulties as their own, and variations in the level of generality at which the sources of difficulty are stated. The level of generality at which the student can recognize his difficulties is important; for if the individual cannot see a difficulty in a general form, he is not likely to be able to apply it to new and specific problems. In some cases the characteristics recognized are trivial and unimportant, while in other cases they are so important as to influence the problem-solving of the individual on both academic and nonacademic problems.

The fourth and following sessions alternated between further analysis and comparison with the protocols of the model students and practice in acquiring the model students' methods of problem-solving. By the end of the fourth session, most of the remedial students were able to discover consistent differences between their methods of problem-solving and those of the model students. All were eager to acquire some of the methods employed by the model students. Again analogizing the learning of the different methods of problem-solving to the learning of a new game, the interviewer pointed out the need for pactice in the new techniques.

The practice was conducted with a booklet, prepared by the Board of Examinations, which contained numerous sample test problems in each of the subject fields. Students also used copies of old examinations and attempted to apply the new methods of problem-solving to a great variety of test problems.

During the practice sessions with the interviewer, which were held approximately twice a week, the students attempted to "think aloud" as they attacked each of the problems. They referred often to their list of differences between themselves and the model students, trying to utilize the general principles inferred from these lists. As a student solved a problem, the interviewer made notes of the student's method and continually asked the student to evaluate his method in relation to what he thought the model student might do with such a problem. It was felt that, until the student could view his own problem-solving objectively, he would not be able to use the problem-solving techniques effectively.

In the training periods, it was stressed that the method of solution rather than the correctness of the answer was important; for it was our hypothesis that, if the student employed a good method, his answers were quite likely to be accurate. This last hypothesis was in part confirmed by the test performance of the original successful problem-solvers whose techniques of problem-solving were being used as models. Much difficulty was experienced in getting the remedial students to focus attention on the method rather than the accuracy of the answers. It must be remembered that most of the previous instruction given these students had placed primary emphasis on the accuracy of the solutions rather than the appropriateness of the process by which the solutions were obtained. We further stressed that the purpose of these practice sessions was not to tutor the student in a particular subject field but rather to provide an opportunity for supervised practice as the student tried to acquire the problem-solving habits of the model student. In addition, students were expected to spend several hours a week in unsupervised practice on the new methods.

One outcome of these sessions was that, as the practice proceeded, it became clear that some specific information was necessary for the solution of the examination problems and that a certain amount of background in the subject field was indispensable. It became apparent that methods of problem-solving, by themselves, could not serve as a substitute for the basic knowledge of the subject matter. Frequently during the practice sessions each student would come upon a question for which he lacked the necessary information, and he would voluntarily look this up before the next practice session. After several such experiences, the students reported that, when they were looking for a particular detail or bit of information as they studied, they had much less difficulty in concentrating. They felt that the problem-solving training was already affecting their study habits. Also, in these practice sessions new difficulties not uncovered in the analysis sessions appeared. When these difficulties were discovered, the student attempted to determine the best method or the method most likely to be used by the model problem-solvers for overcoming them. A check list (see Appendix) of problem-solving difficulties and techniques was compiled at this time from the differences found between the model students and the students in the remedial group. This check list was used to help the student evaluate more systematically any changes in his problem-solving as the practice continued.

Group programs

In later remedial programs the procedure described above was varied somewhat. As can be imagined, a program involving ten or more hours of individual work with one student does not permit work with many students. The development of group techniques, therefore, seemed desirable. The first attempt to introduce group techniques was made with the original remedial group in two of the practice sessions. In these sessions one student would solve the problem aloud while the others took notes on the efficacy of his method. The students compared the attack with that of the model which was read by the experimenter. The notes were then collected and recorded on the blackboard. It was felt that this approach developed a student's ability to make objective observations of problem-solving in others and that it enhanced his ability to observe objectively his own problem-solving methods.

In the summer of 1946 the entire remedial program was carried on in group sessions. The basic procedure here was much the same as in the individual remediation sessions. The first three sessions were devoted to an analysis of the differences in problem-solving methods between the model and the remedial student. The procedure in the group analysis sessions was to flash a typical examination problem on the screen and ask several of the students to solve the problem and to "think aloud" as they did so. Naturally, in these larger group sessions the students tended to be more self-conscious than were the students in individual interviews, and their reports on the process of thought were much less complete. The group then compared the methods of problem-solving used by the several students.

The method of the model student was then presented, and the students were asked to contrast their method of attacking the problem with the model's. They then checked these differences on the Check List on Problem-solving (see Appendix) in tally form, so that the frequency with which each difference occurred could be noted. This check list was a revision of the original check list, compiled on the basis of the differences noted between successful and nonsuccessful students, the model students and the remedial students, and from the characteristics of problem-solving observed in a representative group of students entering the College of the University of Chicago.

The work with groups of students rather than with individuals presented several new considerations in instruction on problem-solving techniques. The groups varied in size from five to twenty students. Working with smaller groups is more nearly like working with individuals and probably is a more effective procedure. It was originally feared that the students might be embarrassed and might not react favorably to participation in a problem-solving group; but, in general, this did not appear to be the case. Most of the students co-operated very well and appeared to be intensely interested in the work.

Supervised practice sessions were initiated in the group after the third analysis session. During these sessions the students practiced in pairs or in small groups. They alternated between attacking problems and observing the problem-solving of other members of the group. When observing, the student attempted to contrast the problem-solving with what he thought the method of the model student would be for a similar problem. The students concentrated on areas where a particular difference between themselves and the model student had occurred frequently, continually referring to the Check List on Problem-solving to note any changes which might be taking place. At times the practice would be concentrated on a particular subject field, with students interested in the same field working together. At other sessions the practice was divorced from subject matter as much as possible, to emphasize greater concentration on method. In such a session, for example, the students worked through the sample-question booklet, reading only directions to the problems and discussing the method to be employed with the particular type of directions.

Of course, some difficulties were experienced owing to the use of group techniques. These were:

1. Little time could be devoted to individual problems. Emphasis was necessarily placed on general areas of difficulty as tabulated from the Check List on Problem-solving.

2. Responsibility for recognizing his own area of difficulty was placed on the student. He recited only a few times during each of the analysis periods, and, if the particular problem discussed did not bring out his major difficulty, it might remain unrecognized. This was compensated for in part by the group practice technique, in which the student had a much greater opportunity to observe the problem-solving behavior of others and the other students might help him to recognize his own difficulties.

3. During the practice sessions the students practiced in pairs or in small groups. In the early practice sessions it was difficult to keep the students' attention on the method of problem-solving rather than on the accuracy of answers, except when they worked under direct supervision. This was, however, less of a problem in the later sessions as the students grew accustomed to the new situation.

4. A few students were unable to work under group conditions. These students were extremely ill at ease and were unable to formulate their thoughts when speaking aloud. In most instances, they voluntarily dropped out of the class. This was rather unfortunate, since it seemed likely they could have been aided by the individual remediation technique.

Our subjective impression of the group techniques in problem-solving indicates that:

1. Problem-solving analysis and practice can be carried on with groups of students, although our experience indicates that twenty students would seem to be the maximum number which can be profitably assigned to one group.
2. Students can recognize their own areas of difficulty in problem-solving and can assume responsibility for directing their efforts toward alleviating these difficulties. They can also recognize these difficulties in others.
3. With respect to holding the attention of the students and their concentrated effort, the group analysis sessions appear to be more effective than the group practice sessions.
4. The students in the group discover the same general areas of difficulty in problem-solving that we observed in the students given individual training in problem-solving.

Changes noted in the problem-solving of the remedial students
A demonstration of the efficacy of a new therapy or remedial program is in large measure dependent upon the appropriateness of the subjects or cases, the skill of the therapist, and the value of the therapy itself. Although we are convinced of the value of the problem-solving remediation, we are not certain that we are skilful in applying the techniques to individual subjects, nor are we certain that we have identified the subjects who can profit most from this type of remediation. Nevertheless, we attempted to secure evidence from a variety of sources, on the effectiveness of the problem-solving remediation.

Much of the evidence is highly subjective, especially that represented by the students' appraisal of the program. Little has been done to quantify the evidence other than that based on examination grades. Because of the conditions under which the comments and appraisals by participants and others were made, there is a strong tendency to secure data only where the change was marked and, to some extent, positive. However, at the outset any new therapy must be considered worthy of further attention if it yields some positive effects and there is no evidence of harmful effects. As skilled operators and appropriate subjects are involved, one can demand more and more rigid tests of the remedial techniques.

1. Evidence from students. — Evidence of change in the problem-solving of the remedial students in several different areas was investigated by the writers. There were, first of all, the verbal reports of the students in the problem-solving group. These reports were inclined to be very optimistic and frequently involved rather extravagant claims. The students, in general, reported increased confidence in themselves and in their ability to take examinations. Several of them also reported increased confidence in their ability to take part in class discussions, indicating more active and more systematic participation on their part. Some of the students reported that they found themselves taking a more critical approach to the analysis of the arguments of others. One student said that, after the problem-solving training, he found himself analyzing his thoughts. He also claimed that he now "thought twice" before taking part in a discussion. Another student,

whose chief difficulty arose from extreme feelings of inferiority and lack of confidence in her own ability (which, in part, appeared to arise from emotional difficulties with her family), reported receiving from a brother a letter which would ordinarily have reduced her to tears. She reported that on this occasion she found herself analyzing his arguments and breaking them down, until her brother's written rebuke no longer had a demoralizing effect upon her.

Several of the students also reported changes in their study habits. One student felt that she was now much more interested in her studies. She had adopted the technique of looking for an answer to a specific question as she studied and found that she was getting a more coherent picture of the assignment she was reading. Another student who had reported difficulty in concentrating as he studied and who had also been inclined to digress to personal considerations during the interview situation gave instances of his increased powers of concentration — he had found that he could study even under such circumstances as when traveling to school.

Some of the students said that other people had noticed changes in them. One student was very pleased to report that both her father and her brother had commented that she seemed to be thinking things through differently. Others indicated that their friends, advisers, and others had commented favorably on the changed ways in which they approached problems.

That the students themselves were pleased with the program and thought it was helping them was further evidenced by the number of students asking to be admitted to the problem-solving remedial sessions on the basis of referrals from students in the group. Some of the students reported that they were trying to help their friends by showing them some of the methods of problem-solving. Many of the students reported, too, that they were greatly encouraged at having been selected for the problem-solving training because they had been discouraged about their failures and had previously felt that the University had taken no interest in them as individuals. As one student expressed it, she finally felt that the "University has a heart."

Further, the faithful attendance records of the students at the problem-solving sessions gave an indication of their interest in, and opinion of, the program, since attendance was not compulsory. Some of the students left their jobs early, and some of them spent as much as three hours in traveling to get to the problem-solving sessions. It must be noted, of course, in connection with the regularity of attendance, that these students were highly motivated by the fact that their enrolment in the College was contingent upon their passing one or more comprehensive examinations at the end of the problem-solving program.

For the most part, the intensive training in problem-solving was discontinued after eight sessions or after the students had taken their first comprehensive examination. After this intensive period of training, many of the students came for further sessions approximately once a month. (This was not true of those students who attended only group sessions.) Changes noted in these students could then be observed over a period of time, and some evidence concerning the permanence of the changes in the problem-solving approach was obtained. One student reported that even after several months she still kept her problem-solving list over the kitchen sink where she could review it daily.

Some of the students' reports of the changes in their problem-solving after six months had elapsed are of interest. In many instances the students ascribed these changes not to the training in problem-solving but to other factors, such as growing older, living in a dormitory, and so on. Helen J. reported:

"In an argument or discussion I find myself arguing logically, point by point. I am glad to think that I can do it. Am more broadminded through comprehensives — I don't pop in and say things until my thoughts are collected. Before, slapped down anything and it didn't matter. Am studying differently. Used to read and outline as I was going through. Too much note-collecting as I went along. Now read through and collect and then go back and outline. Read things over, once to get the general impression, and second to digest the important things. Have a schedule and keep to it. Think the changes are due to dormitory living and the fact that I am emotionally more mature. Now interested in world events, atomic-bomb forums, because of definite views."

Another student, Betty A., when asked what changes she had noted over the six-month period, said:

"More sure of myself. Studying more now than when just out of high school. Didn't know how to study then. Learned the importance of directions. Look for catches, don't do the obvious. Try to understand what to do. In answering multiple-choice question, balance one answer against the other, not taking all at the same time. I see this in my daily life as well as in my problem-solving. Take one thing at a time instead of a finger in every pie. Even my mother has noticed this."

Jean K. reported that after six months she was still conscious of her method. She felt that her problem-solving had been modified. She was still extremely conscious of how a problem should be attacked. She had been applying her problem-solving in conversations with other people and had made some of her friends aware of what they might do to better their problem-solving. She even lent her set of rules to someone. She was of the opinion that the summer's work was very worth while.

The writers realize that the evidence presented cannot be considered truly objective, for in many instances the students were euphoric about the changes they "knew" were taking place. These reports are offered merely as circumstantial evidence that some changes were taking place, even if the changes were only that the students were trying to examine their behavior and reactions in an objective manner.

2. Evidence from members of the faculty. — Evidence from instructors and advisers is difficult to obtain. Since attendance is not compulsory in the College and the roll is not taken, most instructors are not familiar enough with the students in their classes to gather evidence on the types of changes in problem-solving with which we were concerned. Each instructor deals with a large number of students in the lecture hall and in discussion sections and may not even know all his students by name. Again, the student may have a particular instructor for only one quarter, and the instructor would then have little or no opportunity to observe any changes in a student over a period of time. The adviser of a student, who would be in a position to observe the most change, might see the student for perhaps two fifteen-minute periods during the entire three-month quarter. As a result of these conditions, the evidence offered is incomplete. Some of the scattered reports obtainable, however, indicated that a certain degree of change had been

observed in several areas by instructors and advisers.

Several of the students in the problem-solving program were attending a program in remedial reading. This program is designed to increase the speed of reading and to raise the level of comprehension in reading. For a few of these students, the remedial-reading instructor reported that after the problem-solving training their speed of reading had decreased, although their level of comprehension had increased. The problem-solving training was directed, in part, toward increasing the students' understanding of the problem to be solved, and it was recognized that changing the method by which students solved problems would tend to slow down their reasoning. This result reported by the remedial-reading instructor would appear, then, to be some evidence that change was taking place in the desired direction.

The advisers were asked to note any changes in their students as a result of the problem-solving training. They indicated that, on the whole, the most noticeable change in the students after the problem-solving training was their increased confidence in their approach to examinations. The advisers also noted improvement in quarterly and comprehensive examination performance after the problem-solving training. One student in particular, who had a previous record of failures at several schools and who failed three comprehensive examinations at the end of his first year in the College, was titled by his adviser as "the most changed person in the College" after he attended the problem-solving sessions and had received grades of C on the two comprehensive examinations he had retaken.

The students' instructors noted some change in the classroom performance after the problem-solving training. One instructor reported that one student who formerly lacked confidence during classroom discussion and never took an active part had taken the leading role in a discussion for almost the entire period. This same student had been receiving F grades on his examinations but had raised his grades to B in this field after the training. The instructor had observed that this student worked much more slowly and that he did not finish all the problems in his examinations but that he did answer correctly a high proportion of the problems he attempted.

These testimonials from faculty and students seem to afford some evidence that the techniques of problem-solving have carried over to the daily life of the students. The degree of change in these areas cannot be measured, but these reports are offered as further subjective and circumstantial evidence of some of the changes which may in part be attributed to the problem-solving remediation.

3. Evidence from the problem-solving of the students. — In order to secure a somewhat more direct check on the changes taking place in the problem-solving of the remedial students, a set of problems similar in form and in content to those used in the first analysis meeting was prepared. At the last problem-solving meeting, the students were asked to solve these problems and to do so by "thinking aloud." (This analysis was made only for the students who had been given individual problem-solving remediation.) As a result of a comparison of the two sets of solutions to parallel problems, the following general changes were observed:

a) The students read directions more carefully and more completely. There was a definite attempt on the part of all the students to understand the nature of the problem they were to solve before proceeding with the actual solution. They depended less on the question and more on the directions for an understanding of the problem to be solved. Much of the aimless and mechanical reading of directions and problems was eliminated.

b) The students more frequently set up hypotheses as to the correct answer, or set up criteria which the answer must fulfil, before looking at the alternative answers given. In doing this, many of the students attempted to solve the problem without looking at the choice of answers provided, later using the choices supplied as a check on their understanding of the problem and of the accuracy of their solution.

c) In the first analysis session most of the students refused to attack several problems. In the final analysis session they made some attempt to solve each problem, although on several they indicated that they thought the subject matter of the problem was beyond them. They took the attitude that they would attempt to do what they could toward solving the problem with whatever relevant information they had. There was evidence of a change in attitude from a somewhat passive "know or don't know" attitude to a more aggressive approach involving a willingness to try to solve the problem. The students seemed to make some attempt to break into the problem, rather than let the complex appearance of the problem discourage them. Most of the students appeared to feel that no problem was too difficult and that, if they could only attack it properly, they would probably get the correct answer.

d) The comparison of initial and final problem-solving indicated that the students were making a more direct and more systematic attack on the problem. They read the directions, tried to determine just what it was they were to do or to find, and then set about discovering some point for beginning the problem, such as a key word or an example. They tried to set up criteria for an answer and then began a systematic elimination of the choices supplied. As a part of this new and more systematic method of attack, the students attempted to break very complex problems into several simpler subproblems and to make the problem material more concrete.

e) In addition to increased confidence in their ability to attack a given problem, the students seemed to be more confident of the accuracy of the answer they had chosen. The fact that they had done some independent thinking seemed to give them much greater confidence that the solution was correct. The assumption was not always justified, but the confidence remained.

f) The students consciously tried to take a more objective attitude toward the problems. They had, to some extent, developed the ability to start with a problem in its own terms and were less concerned with their own ideas of what was right. An example of this may be seen in the problems where the directions state, "Assume the statements are true." Students who would formerly answer in terms of their own values were now willing to make the assumption as required. They were less frequently led astray by such irrelevant elements as the complexity of the directions, their feelings about the subject field, or the form of the question.

The students also gave evidence of having developed a more objective attitude toward their own problem-solving methods. At the beginning of the practice sessions, many of these students were extremely resistant to the idea of finding differences between themselves and the model students and were concerned only with the accuracy of the answer. In contrast, at the final analysis session they were actively concerned with the fitness of their method and appeared to be much more interested in objectively observing and changing their methods. As they solved a problem during the final analysis period, they occasionally commented on the fitness of the method they were employing.

g) The students tended to do more reasoning about each problem and were able to reason about a particular problem for a longer period of time. They could concentrate on a problem for a longer time than was true at the beginning.

h) When justifying an answer they had selected, the students were more concerned about the adequacy of proof than they had been formerly. Only rarely did they select an answer on the basis of "feeling" or "fitness."

i) They attempted to define or illustrate key technical terms in a question before proceeding to select an answer. This seemed to be a helpful technique for insuring understanding of the problem material.

j) If they had difficulty in dealing with the general or abstract terminology presented in the problem, they reasoned about specific relevant cases and then applied the results of the specific case to the more general case involved in the problem.

Comparison of the original and the final problem-solving records indicated that the students exhibited little or no change in the following areas:

a) Although the students were, in most cases, able to reduce the number of possible answers to two, they were not always able to resolve logically the final choice of the one best answer, and they might introduce personal and value considerations in making this final choice.

b) In general, little headway was made in eliminating the personal and emotional problems of the students which were not directly related to their academic work. This is probably attributable to lack of effort in this direction. We were concerned about only those emotional difficulties which clearly handicapped the student when he attacked specific academic problems.

c) These students still did quite a bit of "free association" as they tried to solve a new problem. They could not emulate the model student's great economy in getting immediately to the heart of a problem and directing all their thinking toward the solution of the problem at hand. They did not appear to be able to do the type of controlled and economical thinking characteristic of the model students. This difference is probably attributable in part to the difference in aptitude between the model and the remedial students.

d) Some of the remedial students still lacked the relevant basic information necessary to the adequate solution of the problem.

4. Evidence of changes in examination performance. — Training of the remedial students in the techniques of problem-solving was carried out in two ways: working with individuals and later (to economize on the amount of time required) working with groups of students. As there was a larger discrepancy between the achievement and the ability of the students working individually than of the students working in groups, somewhat different results might be expected. Results for the two groups, therefore, are reported separately.

a) Changes in performance on comprehensive examinations of students given individual training. -- The students in the first remedial group, which was held during the summer quarter of 1945, took one or more comprehensive examinations at the end of the summer quarter. It was impossible to find matched students having both the same ability (as measured by the entrance tests) and the same achievement (as measured by the comprehensives) who were taking one or more comprehensives at the end of the summer quarter. This difficulty in matching student groups against the first remedial group was due primarily to the fact that students with the same ability as the remedial group did not usually fail so many examinations, while individuals failing the same number of examinations did not usually have the same ability as the original remedial group. The remedial students were, therefore, matched with two separate groups of students: those with the same comprehensive-examination performance and those with similar entrance-test scores. Table 1 shows the comprehensive-examination grades made by the various groups.

It was impossible to find a group of students having identical grades with the remedial group. The thirty letter grades made by the students selected are slightly lower than the thirty-one grades made by the remedial group. On the examinations taken after the problem-solving training, the experimental remedial group more than doubled the proportion of C grades it had made before the training, at the same time reducing the proportion of F grades to less than one-third the proportion made before the training. In contrast, the group matched on the basis of original comprehensive-examination performance did not markedly improve their examination performance. It should be remembered, however, that the matched achievement group had a lower level of scholastic ability than did the experimental students.

Considering the group matched with the remedial group on the basis of aptitude, it is clear that the initial grade performance of the two groups is not equivalent. After the training in problem-solving, the remedial group's achievement more nearly approaches that of the matched aptitude group. However, the remedial students did not quite come up to the achievement level of students with similar scholastic aptitude.

The scholastic aptitude of the remedial group was comparable to that of the College population as a whole. The last column of Table 1 shows the distribution of letter grades on the June, 1945, comprehensive examinations made by the total student population of the College. After the problem-solving training, the remedial students still received about twice as many F grades as would normally be expected, and between two and three times as many D grades. There is also the noticeable lack of A and B grades in the group. There is evidence, however, that the remedial group did show changes in their problem-solving as measured by achievement in the comprehensive examinations. The difference in average grade for the remedial students was significant at the 1 per cent level, while the difference in average grades for the other groups was nonexistent or not significant.

The change in grade average was also extremely important to the remedial students in that the increase now made their grades acceptable for continued enrolment in the College.

b) Changes in performance on comprehensive examinations of students given training in groups. — Table 2 indicates the changes in comprehensive examination performance of students working only in group sessions. Grades up to June, 1946, constitute grades before the problem-solving training, and grades in September, 1946, constitute grades immediately after this training.

TABLE 1

PERCENTAGE DISTRIBUTION OF GRADES MADE ON COMPREHENSIVE EXAMINATIONS BY FIRST EXPERIMENTAL GROUP, TWO MATCHED GROUPS, AND TOTAL GROUP OF COLLEGE STUDENTS

Letter Grade	Point Equiv-alent	Ten Experimental Students		Nine Students Matched on Basis of June, 1945, Grades		Ten Students Matched on Basis of Scholastic Aptitude		Total of College Students
		June, 1945	Sept., 1945	June, 1945	Sept., 1945	June, 1945	Sept., 1945	June, 1945
A	4	...	...	...	...	...	...	11
B	3	...	...	...	...	9	6	19
C	2	26	58	23	29	44	56	54
D	1	22	26	27	18	28	13	9
F	0	52	16	50	53	19	25	7
Total		100	100	100	100	100	100	100
Number of grades		31	19	30	17	32	16	3,396
Average grade points		.74	1.42	.73	.76	1.44	1.44	
Difference in average grade points		+0.68		+0.03		0.00		
Significance of difference		Significant at the 1 per cent level		Not significant		Not significant		

86

TABLE 2

PERCENTAGE DISTRIBUTION OF GRADES, MADE BY STUDENTS TRAINED IN GROUPS, ON COMPREHENSIVE EXAMINATIONS TAKEN BEFORE PROBLEM-SOLVING TRAINING (JUNE, 1946) AND AFTER PROBLEM-SOLVING TRAINING (SEPTEMBER, 1946)

Letter Grade	Point Equivalent	Group 1 — Eleven Students Attending 10-12 Group Meetings		Group 2 — Fourteen Students Attending 7-9 Group Meetings		Group 3 — Eleven Students Attending 4-6 Group Meetings		Group 4 — Eighteen Students Attending 1-3 Group Meetings	
		Grades up to		Grades up to		Grades up to		Grades up to	
		June, 1946	Sept., 1946	June, 1946	Sept., 1946	June, 1946	Sept., 1946	June, 1946	Sept., 1946
A	4	...	4	...	...	...	...	1	...
B	3	2	...	1	...	6	9	6	7
C	2	37	56	36	48	39	29	45	39
D	1	31	32	33	26	27	38	27	26
F	0	30	8	30	26	28	24	21	28
Total		100	100	100	100	100	100	100	100
Number of grades		54	25	73	34	67	21	124	43
Average grade points		1.11	1.60	1.08	1.20	1.22	1.24	1.40	1.26
Difference in average grade points		+0.49		+0.12		+0.02		−0.14	
Significance of difference		Significant at the 2 per cent level		Not significant		Not significant		Not significant	

87

As might have been expected, these results are much less dramatic than those for the individual students. The discrepancy between aptitude and achievement for the students in the group sessions was not so great as for the students in the remedial sessions. Also, the academic achievement of the students in the group sessions was somewhat higher than for the students given individual problem-solving remediation.

The students taking part in the group meetings were divided into four groups, corresponding to the number of problem-solving meetings they had attended. There was a total of twelve meetings, each lasting an hour and a half. The students in Group 1 attended ten, eleven, or twelve of these meetings, constituting all or almost all the series, and would be expected to exhibit greatest change in comprehensive examination performance. Table 2 indicates that they did make the greatest change in achievement. Their difference in the average grade point received is the only one that can be considered statistically significant.

Group 2 consists of those students who attended from seven to nine of the problem-solving group meetings. They might be expected to exhibit less change in academic achievement. The difference in grade point averages by this group is positive but not statistically significant.

Group 3 consists of those students who attended from four to six of the group meetings, which indicates that they missed half, or more than half, of the analysis and practice sessions. Any change in problem-solving would then depend on how much they had absorbed of the techniques in the few sessions they had attended. Table 2 indicates that there was very little change in the performance of these students.

In general, the students in these three groups displayed an increase in the percentage of passing grades (C and D grades) obtained and a decrease in the percentage of failing grades. The percentage of A and B grades did not change significantly in any of these groups.

The fourth group consists of those students attending only one to three meetings. In most cases these were the students who attended one or two of the introductory analysis sessions, and then decided that their difficulties lay in some other area and that the instruction in problem-solving would not benefit them. Their comprehensive-examination achievement decreased slightly in the period of time measured. The difference in average grade-point change is not significant for this group. It will be noted that the initial grade average of Group 4 was the highest of the four groups. This might account for their irregular attendance and the feeling that they did not need problem-solving instruction. However, the highest final grade point average is that of Group 1, their final average exceeding the initial average grade of Group 4.

We may infer, then, that the training in problem-solving does have some effect on the academic achievement of the students as measured by their comprehensive examination performance. For this group of students, at least, the degree of change is related to the amount of time spent in problem-solving instruction. Fewer than nine sessions (thirteen and one-half hours) of group instruction does not appear to be effective in changing performance. This relationship between time spent in remedial problem-solving classes and the degree of change evident suggests that there might also be a personality difference among the students in the four groups, as evidenced by persistence of attendance and interest in the group. This presents an area for further investigation.

Summary

In this chapter on remediation of problem-solving, the writers have attempted to indicate the procedures carried out in working with a group of students whose academic achievement was somewhat lower than might have been predicted from their scholastic aptitude. It was found that, through training in the methods of problem-solving, the achievement of these students could be changed to approach more nearly the expected achievement level.

Evidence of change was obtained from several sources: reports from the students of self-observed differences; reports from members of the faculty about changed classroom behavior, evidence of change in the problem-solving reports given while "thinking aloud," and quantitative changes demonstrated in examination performance. Although much of the evidence is quite subjective, the weight of the evidence is clearly that problem-solving remediation can help students. This approach to remediation appears to be promising for helping failing students in college. The approach is sufficiently general to give some promise as an educational procedure to be used for a much wider range of students than that included in this study.

CHAPTER V

SUMMARY AND DISCUSSION

Processes versus products

In the preceding chapters, we have described some of the results of an exploratory investigation of the problem-solving processes of college students. It is clear that an investigation of processes of thinking does not lend itself to the statistical refinements which characterize investigations of the products of thought. In studies involving such products, it is possible to focus attention on the specific types of information desired, and the data can be classified, analyzed, and summarized in a quantified and objective manner. This is not at present true of studies on the processes of thought. Attempts to describe processes of thinking are comparable in difficulty to attempts to describe a ballet or musical composition in verbal terms. Although much of the work in this study involves attempts to classify processes of thinking, it is recognized that any such system of categorization must result in a loss of much of the essence of the particular process. This difficulty in describing processes of thought is probably just another illustration of the limitations of verbal symbols in describing any processes or activity. As we come to understand more about processes of thought, it is quite likely that a special set of symbols will permit more accurate and efficient description. However, much more must be learned about the thought-processes before we can determine the symbolic system that will best serve our purposes.

A further difficulty in a study of this kind is that of getting from the subject an accurate representation of the process. The subject is not always in a position to describe, or even to know, what his processes of thought are. In many cases the processes take place so quickly that the subject is unable to perceive them. In some cases they probably involve very deep-seated and practically "unconscious" processes, such that the individual does something without knowing what he is doing or how. The subjects available for this investigation were not conversant with introspective techniques, and the data were obtained from them after a very brief training period on the methods of thinking aloud. Perhaps more complete and accurate descriptions of the processes might be obtained from subjects trained in introspective techniques. The method of thinking aloud served, however, to yield relatively consistent and meaningful data from the majority of the subjects. In a few subjects it appeared to be the ideal technique for securing information about their processes of thought. It is possible that, with some refinements, the method can be made a very satisfactory technique for securing this type of evidence from most subjects.

As has been emphasized elsewhere, investigations of thought-processes can be of great value in determining the relationship between products of thought and processes of thought and in answering certain questions about these relationships. To what extent are particular products or solutions produced by a variety of mental processes? To what extent does the student

90

blunder through to the correct solution? Do our present measures of achievement and aptitude, which are expressed in terms of accuracy of solutions and speed of response, reflect the quality of the examinee's thinking? The quality of problem-solving processes may be thought of in terms of the efficiency with which an individual arrives at a solution, the extent to which he brings in extraneous material and ideas, the extent to which he is swayed by considerations external to the problem itself, and the extent to which he can pursue a particular line of attack until he has exhausted its possibilities. If we can find a high correspondence between accuracy of products and quality of processes of thought, then, by all means, we should place major emphasis on the more easily obtained products. If, however, there is not a one-to-one relationship between products and processes, as seems to be the case, evidence on one should be supplemented by evidence on the other.

Variations in students

In chapter ii of this study we described some of the variations among students in ways of attacking problems. These variations were categorized in some detail under the major headings, "Understanding of the Nature of the Problem," "Understanding of the Ideas Contained in the Problem," "General Approach to the Solution of Problems," and "Attitude toward the Solution of Problems." These categorizations, although rough, appear to give some insight into the ways in which students differ. It should be recognized that we have attempted to describe only the ways in which a relatively homogeneous group of college students in a single institution differ. These techniques should be somewhat more effective in differentiating individuals in groups which are more heterogeneous with regard to such characteristics as intelligence, age, class and cultural level, educational grade level, and type of subject-field specialization.

A study of variations in students' processes of problem-solving should be of value in diagnosing individual difficulties. Here one can determine not only the kinds of difficulties a person has but, to some extent, the sources of these difficulties. Such data are likely to be of value in predicting later success in problem-solving, especially as it is reflected in educational and other types of achievement. Perhaps an even more important value of a study of variations in problem-solving processes is its use as a basis for planning educational experiences. Such experiences may be planned to remedy specific difficulties of individual students or to remedy the most common difficulties of a group of students. Still another way in which this planning may take place is the determination of the ways in which those educational experiences might best be organized and handled.

Another possible use of a study of variations in the problem-solving processes of students is the measurement of change as the result of certain educational experiences. The kinds of data on the products of thinking which we now secure by testing techniques are relatively crude. On a test of a hundred points, we usually find that a group of students have gained about a half-dozen points after a year of intensive study of a subject. Growth studies with achievement tests usually reveal considerable overlap in the initial and retest scores of a group of students. In spite of this evidence of relatively little change, teachers and students are frequently of the opinion that great change has taken place in the students' abilities, skills, and habits. There is some hope that an investigation of changes in the processes of problem-solving may reveal that educational experiences do produce greater and more fundamental changes than are at present reflected in our measures of academic achievement — especially if such educational experiences are carefully planned and skilfully organized. It is true that attempts to secure evidence on growth or change in processes of thinking will involve costly and difficult investigations. However, until we have fully explored some of these possibilities, we are hard pressed to justify present educational methods, the elaborate school systems, and the tremendous expenditures of student and faculty time if the typical study on growth in products of thinking is an accurate representation of the changes which really take place.

Still another way in which the study of variations in students' processes of problem-solving may be of value is in furthering an understanding of the individual student. Our systems of mass education result in more and more distant relationships between teacher and student. The individual student becomes only another unit in a large educational system, and his instructors know little about him. If a teacher can get to know more about the individual's processes of thinking (as well as many other kinds of data about him), this should do much to alter the relationships between teacher and student. It is not in the province of this paper to discuss all the ways in which we might get to know and understand the student. It does seem likely, however, that evidence on the thought-processes in problem-solving can give us greater and greater insight into the individual — his needs, his problems, and his sources of difficulty.

Variations in problems

In chapter iii of this monograph we discussed some of the ways in which academic problems differ in the problem-solving processes they evoke. An attempt was made to describe some of the primary sources of difficulty students had with specific problems, as well as the methods of attack they used on particular problems. As we get to know more about what is required by a specific kind of problem, we can secure greater control in the development of problems which will require the particular processes in which we are interested.

A study of variations in problems should be of value for the teacher. The teacher assigns many problems to the individual but is never quite certain what each problem requires and what kinds of behavior or thinking it elicits from the student. As some of the primary problems in a particular subject field are investigated by problem-solving studies, we can begin to determine what the sources of difficulty are in specific problems, the kinds of mental processes evoked by each type of problem, and the types of training which will best prepare students to attack and solve these problems. The teacher who engages in problem-solving studies of this kind, or who takes time to learn the results of problem-solving studies in his field, should be in a better position to plan and organize the educational experiences which will prepare students to attack the major kinds of problems in that subject field.

The new teacher or the student teacher often has great difficulty in comprehending the sources of difficulty students will have with particular problems. Such teachers are often more engrossed in the subject matter than in the relations between the subject matter and the student. Rather simple investigations could be organized whereby an apprentice teacher would identify some of the major kinds of problems in his subject field and then study the problem-solving processes of a small representative group of students. The writers explored this kind of investigation with a small number of graduate students in the Department of Education at the University of Chicago. Each of the students identified a dozen or more kinds of problems in connection with his subject field and then attempted to study the thought-processes of a small group of subjects in connection with these problems. In each case the student was of the opinion that he had gained much insight into the subject matter as well as into the considerations to be kept in mind in the teaching of that subject. This type of investigation might well be carried on as a project in connection with courses in educational psychology or courses in the teaching of a particular subject field.

Another value of studies of variations in problems is in connection with the construction of tests. At present, testing procedures are based largely on the results of statistical investigations or on operational definitions of the types of behavior to be measured. If examinations are based on statistical techniques, we usually are satisfied with less elaborate definitions of the behavior being measured and are primarily concerned with the extent to which a particular sample of behavior is predictive of other indexes of behavior, such as teacher judgment and later performance in a particular field. Procedures such as this give very little control over test construction. In essence, what is done is to construct a large number of test situations and then retain those which empirical results indicate are best.

Another approach to test construction has been the attempt to obtain explicit definitions of a behavior to be measured, to construct test problems and situations which appear to represent this behavior, and then to use expert opinion to determine whether the test situations are really appropriate to the defined behavior. Under this method, we get no evidence on the student and what he does in the test situation. In the opinion of the writers, we can never really be certain that a test situation is appropriate to a particular definition of behavior until we have observed the actual behavior of the student when confronted with the test situation. The general steps in test construction and validation would then be:

1. Secure explicit definitions of the behavior to be measured.
2. Develop test situations which presumably are appropriate.
3. Present the test situations to students while various observations are being made — especially observations on the processes of thought involved.
4. Use expert opinion to determine whether the behavior evoked by the test situation really reflects the defined behavior which the test situation was to have measured.

This method of validating tests was recently explored with relatively satisfactory results by Lingenfelder (10) in the development of achievement tests for advanced students in education. Studies such as these should give a great deal of control in the preparation of test problems. They should help us to predict the kind of behavior a particular test exercise is likely to elicit.

Remedial measures

Educational institutions appear to be satisfied with a higher proportion of failures than almost any other kind of organization or institution. Only about one-third of the students who enter a typical college ever graduate.

Although many students drop out because of financial difficulties, competition of other interests, and changes in the students' plans, a large proportion leave because of failure or near-failure in academic work. In chapter iv of this monograph we described a technique for aiding failing students and presented some results obtained by the use of this technique. We are of the opinion that these methods are relatively crude and do not, as yet, give much control over changes in the students' achievement. This study, however, was promising enough to indicate the value of basing remedial measures for failing students on an investigation of their problem-solving processes. Such remedial training should be of great value in reclaiming student failures. On the basis of the results reported here, it should be possible, in a relatively small amount of time, to alter a student's method of attacking problems and to increase his success in solving them.

However, as we have used the technique, it would seem to be almost too late. We used these remedial measures only after the student had given ample evidence of failure. Such measures would seem to be much more valuable if they were used long before the student had to suffer the frustrating and discouraging experiences of academic failure. It would be desirable to identify probable failures as early in their academic careers as possible and then to train these students in more effective techniques of problem-solving. Scholastic-aptitude predictors are accurate enough to enable us to identify a large proportion of the prospective failures long before they have had the opportunity to fail.

Still another value of remedial measures in problem-solving processes is in connection with the orientation to particular academic courses or the beginning of a large unit of educational experiences. Some students seem to spend much time in "finding" themselves. During this orientation period they use ineffective ways of attacking problems and have difficulty in developing effective study habits. It would seem desirable to begin a course with some instruction on the methods of attacking problems peculiar to its subject field. This technique should result in an increase in the effectiveness of both the student and the teacher. It should also result in a reduction in the proportion of failures or near-failures in the course.

The preceding section represents a brief summary of the investigations reported in chapters i through iv of this monograph. These investigations were exploratory rather than definitive in nature, and they were more productive of problems and questions than of answers. Many specific problems were raised and discussed in each of the chapters. In the following section, some major generalizations about problem-solving processes are discussed. These generalizations are presented as hypotheses which might be further investigated.

Some major hypotheses for research

As the "thinking-aloud," problem-solving records of students are analyzed, it becomes increasingly evident that the processes involved have a definite form and structure. It is possible to draw certain generalizations which characterize the mental operations of most of the students in the type of problem-solving included in this study. The generalizations, once stated, appear to be obvious, but perhaps their obvious nature is further evidence of their validity.

Although the generalizations may be known at a "common-sense" level, little is known about the more precise quantitative and qualitative differences among individuals with respect to them. In addition, present educational procedures evidently do not recognize, or make use of, these generalizations about the problem-solving processes. Generalizations such as those presented in the following material should be of value in planning further experimentation and study in this field. They constitute tentative working hypotheses which may be used as a basis for the design of experiments and as a stimulus to the development of new techniques of research on the problem-solving processes.

It must be emphasized again that the generalizations are based on scanty data obtained under inadequately controlled conditions. They represent little more than an attempt to focus attention on some lines of investigation which should prove fruitful. They should serve to raise questions which more definite studies must answer. There is much need for the development of ingenious and imaginative methods of research on mental processes. This is an area which could profit greatly from co-operative research, involving specialists in such divergent fields as education, psychology, sociology, anthropology, physiology, and philosophy. A sound research program on the nature of the mental processes involved in problem-solving should be of great value in the discovery of means of changing mental processes which will make possible the development of more rational and effective individuals.

Tension and relaxation. — In working with various students, it became apparent that some of them developed great tension as they became involved in the attack on a problem. This tension was usually relieved when they found a solution to the problem. The tension appeared to be a physical phenomenon and seemed to be most clearly related to the neck and facial muscles, to the stomach muscles, and to the rate and depth of breathing. In some cases the tension appeared to be fairly great, and the relaxation from it seemed to afford much relief to the individual.

It was noted that the greatest tension appeared to be produced when the individual attempted to solve a very complex problem. For such problems, a solution which the individual thought to be correct, or a solution which was based on what the individual considered to be a good method of problem-solving, seemed to produce the most complete relaxation. Thus, the amount of tension and relaxation appeared to be directly related to the amount of mental effort exerted on the problem and the amount of confidence the individual had in the solution. When the student attacked a very difficult problem but had no confidence in the solution he found, or when he gave up the attack before arriving at a solution, there seemed to be little immediate relaxation. In such cases the tension seemed to last for a relatively long period after the particular problem had been set aside.

Little tension or corresponding relaxation seemed to be produced when the problem was very easy for the student or when the solution was a remembered one rather than one derived from the particular problem at hand. Little or no tension seemed to be produced when the individual made only a slight effort to attack a problem or when the individual selected an answer as a matter of random guess. Thus, when little mental effort was expended, little tension was produced.

The effects of tension may be seen in the following illustration. In one of the problems attacked by a group of students, the task was to assemble a number of cut-out pieces of wood in such a way that they would represent a hand. The pieces were placed on the table in a random manner, and the students did not, at first, recognize what the final object would be. In this experimental presentation of the problem, the students were asked to do the entire task mentally rather than manipulate the pieces. Several of the students, after a fair amount of mental effort, recognized that the pieces formed a hand. As soon as this was recognized, their initial tension appeared to have been dissipated, and it took some prodding to induce them to complete the task, which was that of determining the final relationships among the pieces. That is, the relaxation occurred as soon as the students had reached one solution although this was not the final solution called for in the problem. The dissipation of the tension appeared to handicap further effort at completing the problem. Such relaxation from tension apparently may occur when a solution is seen but not necessarily reached, or when an incorrect solution, which the subject regards as correct, is reached.

It would appear that some tension is necessary to keep the thoughts centered on the problem at hand. Thus, when individuals were asked to relax as much as possible while a problem was read to them, they seemed to be unable to organize the problem, and the statement of the problem seemed to be just so many words. The reader will undoubtedly remember many instances of attempting to read while in a very relaxed state. In such a state he probably found that many words were read with little or no grasp of the ideas involved.

Tension also appears necessary to secure production of what might be called "controlled association." Thus, as the mind goes from one idea to related ideas, tension appears to be one factor governing the extent to which the ideas are related to the problem at hand. When tension is not present as an individual works with a problem, a whole host of free associations may come to the consciousness. One might conceive of the individual as holding back a great stream of ideas, relevant and irrelevant, as long as a certain amount of tension is present. When tension is eliminated, this control is broken and, in effect, a dam of ideas is released.

Perhaps this point can be best illustrated by an example. The following problem was read to a subject: "If a man buys seven two-cent stamps and gives the postal clerk a half-dollar, how much change should he get back?"

Before the problem was read, one of the subjects was told to relax as much as possible. As the problem was read, he began to think about a post-office clerk. In this case the subject "thought aloud" of the post-office clerk as a little, fat man with eccentric mannerisms; from there he thought about the post office in which this clerk worked; from there to a well-remembered post office in his home town; and then to some of the people he had associated with in his home town. As he relaxed, the subject drifted away from the problem at hand — that of figuring out change — and began to think about all the things which were related to a particular and unessential phrase in the problem. In effect, the problem became merely a steppingstone toward a great many ideas, most of which were not relevant to the problem at hand.

Although there is little evidence on the subject, it appears quite likely that, while too little tension may be detrimental to the solution of a problem, too great a tension may be just as strong an inhibiting factor for problem-solving. A number of the students reported that their minds "went blank" during final examinations. In these cases a great deal of nervous tension appeared to be present.

The evidence for the tension and relaxation is not based on well-controlled experiments and observations. One source of the hypotheses given above was a limited study of the physiological reactions of four subjects while they attempted to solve a number of problems. Polygraph records (galvanic skin response, pulse rate, blood pressure, breathing rate, and finger tremor) were made while synchronized recordings were made of the subjects' "thinking aloud" as they attacked a problem. However, the major source was the subjective impressions of fairly competent observers and subjects. Much must still be done to secure more objective evidence as to the state of tension and relaxation under varying problem-solving situations. It is hoped that problem-solving experiments can be conducted in which both introspective and retrospective impressions of the subject are secured while the appropriate physiological measurements are made. Such experiments should be carried out with problems from a variety of subject fields, as well as with problems varying in difficulty.

The tentative results reported here on tension are, in general, in agreement with previous research in this field. Bills (2), in summarizing the literature on facilitation and inhibition in mental work, reports that most studies find some increase of muscular tension accompanying any augmentation in mental effort. However, on the crucial question as to whether mental effort can occur without an increase in tension and whether induced tension has a dynamogenic effect on mental processes, there is conflicting evidence. The literature supplies little evidence on the optimum amount of tension for various kinds of problems or on the relation between success or failure and speed and extent of relaxation.

The production of tension and relaxation appears to have especially important implications for education. Insofar as the writers are able to ascertain, the relaxation from the tension is a very welcome and even enjoyable feeling. The building-up of tension produces some discomfort, but the relaxation appears to more than compensate for this discomfort. It is quite probable that some of the enjoyment individuals get from mental effort is directly associated with this tension and relaxation. Any person who has attacked a difficult problem which has bothered him for some time will remember the wonderful and pleasing effect of finding a solution. Perhaps the lack of tension and relaxation for certain individuals may explain why they avoid problem-solving to a large extent. If, as indicated above, relaxation does not take place when the individual has little confidence in his solution, or if little tension and relaxation are produced when the problem requires little mental effort, we may see why many individuals do not get pleasure from problem-solving. It is possible that this tension and relaxation effect may explain why so many individuals secure pleasure from jigsaw puzzles, crossword puzzles, and radio-quiz problems. If this is true, then a major problem for education is to determine how individuals can get the same pleasure from the somewhat more real and important problems which the school may pose for them.

If people are to get pleasure from thinking, they should, it would seem, find both tension and relaxation in problem-solving. If education is to induce individuals to do much thinking, as well as to enjoy such thinking, it would appear necessary to find ways in which students can secure both tension and relaxation. One requirement for this is to give the students problems at an appropriate level of difficulty such that they can arrive at solutions in which they can be confident. A good type of problem might be a very large and complex one which could be divided into subproblems in such a way that, as the student attacks and solves each subproblem, he gets alternation of feelings of tension and relaxation until he has finally attacked and solved the total problem.

This brief discussion of the physiological accompaniments of problem-solving is not intended to suggest that the end of problem-solving is represented by physiological reactions. The mental activities of problem-solving appear to be accompanied by certain easily observed physiological changes. Such physiological changes may accompany work on important or trivial problems, effective or ineffective methods of problem-solving, and good or poor solutions. These changes must be taken into consideration, but they do not, in themselves, suggest desirable problem-solving techniques, nor do they constitute the important outcomes of problem-solving.

Foreground-background. -- As an individual gives attention to a problem and the materials in it, certain aspects and details appear to stand out and occupy the foreground of attention, as contrasted with a background consisting of the other aspects and details which are given little or no attention. Insofar as can be determined, the individual's conception of the problem and his insight into the nature of relevant materials determine, to a large degree, what comes to the foreground.

Perhaps what is meant by this foreground-background relationship can best be illustrated by a brief experiment. In this experiment the students were told they would be permitted to see a picture for several seconds, and they were asked to note the colors included in the picture. After the picture was exposed to their view for this brief period of time, the subjects were able to name the colors in the picture but were able to remember very few of the other details in the picture. In another experiment under similar conditions, when the subjects were asked to note the details in the picture, they were able to remember a great many of the specific details but were unable to name many of the colors included. In still a third experiment the subjects were asked to count the number of objects of a particular type in the picture (in one they were asked to note the number of boats, while in another they were asked to note the number of windows in the building pictured). Here, again, the subjects were able to recall the particular details to which their attention had been directed but were quite unaware of most of the other details in the picture.

The basis of organization given to the students seemed to determine, to a large extent, which details or portions of the picture came to the foreground and which remained in the background. The extent to which the students noted details other than those called for in the problem appeared to be a function of the difficulty in grasping the details called for, as well as the amount of time they were permitted to study the picture. It appears to be possible to design problems in such a way that two groups of subjects will note entirely different details or content, although presented with identical material.

When individuals were directed to think aloud as they attacked various examination problems, this foreground-background relationship was again evident. Some individuals would read the problem and omit certain key words as they read the problem the first time. As they encountered difficulty, they reread the problem and repeatedly omitted the same key words. It seemed that, unless their attention was called to it specifically, the individuals were unable to bring different material in the problem to the foreground. Other evidence on this foreground-background relationship may be seen in the extent to which the individual was unable to get out of a "rut" as he worked a problem over and over, repeatedly making the same errors.

As the students were observed, it became evident that they differed in the speed with which the foreground-background relationship was established and that there were differences from one type of problem to another. Some individuals appeared to convert the problem and its material into that to be focused on and that to be placed in the background as they read the problem. Some students appeared to anticipate the problem and, even before they had completed the reading, seemed to bring certain materials to the foreground. This selection and focusing was evident in the ways in which certain words were emphasized or omitted as the student read the problem. Other individuals appeared to establish the foreground-background relationship very slowly, rereading the problem and the materials in it over and over again until something appeared to "click." In some cases the individual never could seem to reduce the problem or to focus on particular details in it.

Individuals also appeared to differ in the strength of the foreground-background relationship which they established. Some students seemed almost completely unable to change the relationship once it was established. For them the problem had assumed a particular and specific form which no amount of effort appeared to alter. These students would read and reread the problem many times but seemed unable to change it or to see it in a different way. Other students seemed able to look at the problem and its material in one way; then, if they encountered difficulty, they were able to start the problem again almost as a new problem and to focus on different material. That is, they seemed able to start the problem with one foreground-background relationship, then start again on the problem and secure a different foreground-background relationship. This would appear to be evidence that the strength of the first foreground-background relationship was not so great as to interfere with the formation of a new relationship based on the same materials.

Individuals also appeared to differ in the breadth of detail encompassed in the foreground. Some appeared able to bring relatively little material to the foreground, while others appeared to make use of a great wealth of detail and material. This was most evident in the pictures, where some individuals were able to see and remember a great many things in the picture, while others were able to see and remember only a small number of details. In the verbal problems some students were able to hold a great many elements in mind and to use them in working the problem, while others appeared to be conscious of relatively few elements as they attacked the problem.

Individuals differed in the extent to which they brought relevant details to the foreground. Some individuals persistently brought irrelevant material to the foreground and were unable to solve the problems successfully. The basis they used for selecting material seemed to have little value for the particular problem. In some cases this irrelevance and lack of value of the material was attributable to emotional factors; in other cases it appeared to be due to lack of familiarity with the type of problem or lack of knowledge of the essential ideas involved. Other individuals appeared to be able to bring to the foreground the optimum amount of relevant material. They seemed to select for the foreground only those materials which were most useful in solving the problem.

It is difficult at present to determine the relative value of speed, strength, breadth, and relevance in the development of foreground-background relationships. Other things being equal, it would seem that the greater the speed with which the relationship is established, the narrower the foreground and the greater the background. On simple and straightforward problems, rapid establishment of foreground-background relationships would appear to give great economy and efficiency in problem-solving. That is, the problems could be solved with little attention to irrelevant material. On more complex problems, if the speed reduced the amount of material considered in the foreground, there is greater likelihood of difficulty in solving the problem correctly, since many of the essential elements may not be included in the foreground. Thus, if a problem is really complex, one might do well to develop the foreground slowly, from great breadth to a narrower and narrower foreground, until gradually the focus comes to a point that involves all the essential elements and none of the unessential.

Since the strength of the foreground-background relationship is defined in terms of the ease with which it can be altered, it would appear that a strong relationship would tend to make it more economical to work on the foreground material, since there would be little fluctuation in its content. However, on complex problems, this very strength makes it hard for the individual who encounters difficulties to overcome them, since he cannot get a really fresh start on the problem after he has attempted to attack it the first time.

With respect to foreground-background relationships, the problem of education would seem to be one of helping the individual develop control of the speed, strength, breadth, and relevance of the foreground. It appears to be one of enabling the student to approach a problem from a number of different viewpoints so that the most useful foreground-background relationships may be established. If the student is to do any really creative work, he must be able to collapse one foreground-background relationship that did not prove to be fruitful and start again with different relationships, until the right combination is finally secured. Another problem for education is that of getting the student to narrow the foreground material as he becomes more and more certain that he is on the right course.

Insofar as foreground-background is concerned, the problem of examination construction would seem to be one of setting problems in a way that will require the student to exhibit a great range of speed, strength, breadth, and relevance in his foreground-background relationships. One criterion of the adequacy of a test might be the types of foreground-background relationships demanded by it. Perhaps the student might be given problems in which one foreground-background relationship is established and then he is required to alter it and produce a different relationship. Still other problems might be set up in such a way as to present the student with an overwhelming amount of detail from which he might be expected to develop a relatively narrow foreground.

The problem of changing attitudes and emotions would, on this basis, appear to be one of weakening certain foreground-background relationships now existing and building up new ones. Thus, if an individual is able to take only a biased and narrow view of the characteristics of Negroes, Jews, or members of some other minority group, the problem of changing attitudes in this area would then seem to be one of discovering what characteristics the individual now sees and then either destroying this foreground or taking other details (characteristics of the minority group not seen at present by the individual) and adding them to the foreground. In altering the foreground, it might be necessary to get the individual to attempt to forget everything he now knows about the minority group and then bring to the foreground a more truly representative picture.

Much must be learned about foreground-background relationships. We must learn how such relationships are developed and the kinds of educational experiences which will alter them. It would appear desirable to set up criteria which will yield an index of the speed, strength, breadth, and relevance of foreground development for different individuals and for different problems. Another task is that of setting up problems, experiments, and techniques which will enable investigators to study each of the characteristics of foreground-background relationships discussed here. In what ways do the foreground-background relationships affect the accuracy of problem-solving? In what ways do they affect the originality of the solutions obtained? The Gestalt concept of figure-ground would appear to be closely related to the concept of foreground-background relationships. A tentative distinction between the two concepts is that the figure-ground concept has been largely confined to perceptual problems, while the foreground-background relationships discussed here apply to all types of academic problems. Further research will be needed to establish whether the generalizations about perceptual figure-ground relationships also apply to the thought-processes involved in problem-solving.

In this discussion it is emphasized that individuals select from the materials given in a problem those elements which are to be given primary attention and those elements which are to be given little or no attention. This differential attention has appeared in every problem included in this study, and the variations from student to student in this respect serve to explain some of the individual differences in problem-solving.

Key points. — As we observe students attacking a variety of problems, it is quite evident that some points in a problem seem to furnish a starting point for students to a much greater extent than do others. Thus, if one can conceive of the statement of a problem as involving as many as a hundred elements, it will be noted that students will begin their attack on only a very small number of these elements. It is safe to say that only a fourth or fewer of the elements in a problem are used frequently as the key points or the points of departure in attacking the problem. The presence of such key points should be investigated fairly thoroughly to determine the qualities which make for key points and to discover why some students select one type of key point for starting the problem while other students select other key points. What in the problem determines that certain elements will be used in beginning the attack while others will not? Is it possible to predict in advance what points will be used as keys?

The presence of key points may most easily be seen in block-design problems. Here, when the subjects are asked to assemble a dozen blocks in such a way as to form a design, the students usually begin by starting at one of a few points in the design and very infrequently begin at other points. The point at which they begin seems to be an outstanding part of the design, or the key to a particular motif in the design. If the design is one which involves the recurrence of a particular pattern, the students seem to find it necessary to complete one pattern and then simply to reproduce it as many times as the design calls for.

In another test the subject is required to arrange a series of pictures in the most logical sequence. Although this particular test consists of four pictures, all the students tested appeared to start with a particular picture and then to build the sequence around that. One wonders why students so rarely started with other pictures as the point of departure.

As the students were observed, it was apparent that certain characteristics determined the key points. Although the evidence is not very clear or complete on this, it is possible to identify three of the more obvious characteristics of key points.

1. If the problem contains unfamiliar terms or terms of which the student is uncertain, there is some attempt to dispose of these terms before proceeding to the remainder of the problem. Thus, if the term is unfamiliar or quite abstract, the student will attempt to define it in some way, sometimes by actually citing a particular definition, in other cases by translating the term into more familiar or more concrete terms. When the student is unable to define a term with any degree of confidence, he will frequently assume that for the purposes of this problem he will operate as though the term meant a particular thing, which he will then state. Although this assumption is often incorrect, the student seems to have increased confidence in his ability to solve a problem when he makes such an assumption. If the student does not have any clues as to what the term means, he will frequently omit it entirely. He will express some concern about the term but will, in effect, say, "Since I do not know what this term means, I will work the problem as though the term were not present."

No attempt is made here to indicate what is the best way to deal with unfamiliar terms. The main idea is that the student finds it necessary to dispose of these terms before proceeding further, and for him these become key points, even though the term itself may be relatively unimportant in the problem. It would be desirable to experiment further with the effect of such unfamiliar terms in problem-solving and to determine why students most frequently begin with these terms before attempting a further attack on the problem.

2. If the problem involves position, the point which stands out most will be used as the starting point. This is a perceptual phenomenon of which advertising writers and illustrators make excellent use; that is, some aspects of the problem assume a very definite figure relation, while the remaining material assumes a ground relation. This was especially evident in the figure-design problem, in which the student most frequently started with certain positions of the design as his key or starting point. It is quite likely that some of these outstanding points are not really the most efficient points at which the problem should be started, that their outstanding characteristics do not necessarily lend themselves to serving as the real keys and clues to the solution of the problem. It would be desirable to set up problems in which the characteristics of such points actually inhibit the solution of the problem and to find the effect of this figure-ground relationship in promoting and retarding an efficient attack on a problem.

3. If the criteria for the solution are not clearly evident in the problem,

the students frequently begin with a quick enumeration of such criteria, perhaps as a method of delimiting the problem. That is, if the problem is not fully given, the student will attempt to circumscribe and delimit it in such a way that he will know when he has arrived at a solution. It should be pointed out here that this was the method most frequently used by the so-called "model" students and is not necessarily characteristic of students who have great difficulty in problem-solving. The use of such criteria as the key points in an attack on the problem seems to make the attack more economical and helps the individual to come more quickly to the solution.

A concluding word

This monograph reports an exploratory investigation of problem-solving processes on a limited number and variety of academic problems. The methods used have been relatively crude, and there are many restrictions to be placed on the results. We are convinced, however, that a study of problem-solving processes is basic to an understanding of individual differences — their measurement and control. The development of more refined techniques of getting evidence on the processes of thinking, the creation of a symbolic system for representing the processes, and the discovery of a set of criteria to insure adequacy of sampling of problems are necessary tools which must be perfected before research in this field can be greatly improved or stabilized. Systematic research in this psychological field should yield results fundamental to a qualitative as well as quantitative science of human behavior.

BIBLIOGRAPHY

1. Billings, Marion Leroy. "Problem-solving in Different Fields of Behavior," American Journal of Psychology, XLVI (April, 1934), 259-72.
2. Bills, Arthur G. "Facilitation and Inhibition in Mental Work," Psychological Bulletin, XXXIV (May, 1937), 286-309.
3. Buswell, G. T., with the co-operation of Lenore John. Diagnostic Studies in Arithmetic. Supplementary Educational Monographs, No. 30. Chicago: University of Chicago Press, 1926.
4. Dewey, John. How We Think: A Restatement of the Relation of Reflective Thinking to the Educative Process. New York: D. C. Heath & Co., 1933.
5. Heidbreder, E. F. "Problem-solving in Children and Adults," Pedagogical Seminary and Journal of Genetic Psychology, XXXV (December, 1928), 522-45.
6. Hildreth, Gertrude. "Puzzle-solving with and without Understanding," Journal of Educational Psychology, XXXIII (November, 1942), 595-604.
7. Judd, Charles Hubbard, with the co-operation of Ernst R. Breslich, J. M. McCallister, and Ralph W. Tyler. Education as Cultivation of the Higher Mental Processes. New York: Macmillan Co., 1936.
8. Köhler, Wolfgang. The Mentality of Apes. New York: Harcourt, Brace & Co., 1927.
9. Lapp, C. J. "The Effectiveness of Problem Solving in Producing Achievement in College Physics," American Journal of Physics, IX (August, 1941), 239-41.
10. Lingenfelder, Louise M. "The Development of Methods for Constructing a Diagnostic and Placement Examination over the General Field in Education." Unpublished Doctor's dissertation, Department of Education, University of Chicago, 1947.
11. MacLatchy, Josephine H. "Variety in Problem-solving," Education, LXI (April, 1941), 453-57.
12. Maier, Norman R. F. "An Aspect of Human Reasoning," British Journal of Psychology, XXIV (October, 1933), 144-55.
13. Maier, Norman R. F. "Reasoning in Children," Journal of Comparative Psychology, XXI (June, 1936), 357-66.
14. Morgan, C. Lloyd. An Introduction to Comparative Psychology. New York: Charles Scribner's Sons, 1898.
15. O'Neill, Hugh P., S.J. "Toward Mental Efficiency," School and Society, LIII (January 11, 1941), 51-54.
16. Parker, Samuel Chester. "Problem-solving or Practice in Thinking," Elementary School Journal, XXI (September, October, November, and December, 1920), 16-25, 98-111, 174-88, 257-72.
17. Piaget, Jean. Judgment and Reasoning in the Child. New York: Harcourt, Brace & Co., 1928.
18. Polya, György. How To Solve It. Princeton, New Jersey: Princeton University Press, 1945.

BIBLIOGRAPHY

19. Thorndike, Edward Lee. Animal Intelligence: Experimental Studies. New York: Macmillan Co., 1911.
20. Titchener, Edward Bradford. Lectures on the Experimental Psychology of the Thought Processes. New York: Macmillan Co., 1909.
21. Wertheimer, Max. Productive Thinking. New York: Harper & Bros., 1945.

CHECK LIST ON PROBLEM-SOLVING

Name _____ Year of the College _____ Date _____

(Frequency)			
YES	NO	**I. UNDERSTANDING OF THE NATURE OF THE PROBLEM**	Comments

A. Ability to start the problem (comprehension of directions)
  1. Re-reads directions aimlessly — does not concentrate sufficiently to understand directions on first reading.
  2. Lacks understanding of the terms and phrases in the directions.
  3. Depends on the questions rather than the directions for an understanding of the nature of the problem.

B. Ability to understand the specific problem presented
  1. Has difficulty as a result of improper reading of directions.
    a) Makes no attempt to read the directions.
    b) Misreads the directions.
    c) Misinterprets the directions.
    d) Reads directions incompletely.
    e) Reads directions too rapidly.
  2. Forgets or loses sight of the directions.

C. Other difficulties

II. UNDERSTANDING OF THE IDEAS CONTAINED IN THE PROBLEM

A. Ability to bring relevant knowledge to bear on the problem
  1. Possesses little or no knowledge about the ideas contained in the problem.

APPENDIX

(Frequency) YES	NO	II. (Continued)	Comments

<table>
<tr><td>YES</td><td>NO</td></tr>
</table>

(Frequency)
YES   NO

II. (Continued)   Comments

2. Is unable to realize fully the implications
   of the ideas.
3. Is unable to use whatever relevant knowledge is possessed because of the presence of unfamiliar terms and ideas.

B. Ability to comprehend the ideas in the form
   presented in the problem
   1. Is unable to translate the difficult and ab-
      stract terms of the problem into simpler
      and more concrete terms or into more
      familiar terms.
   2. Is unable to visualize some of the ideas.
   3. Has difficulty in grasping the ideas at the
      first reading (necessitating rereading).
   4. Works too rapidly to secure an under-
      standing of the problem.

III. GENERAL APPROACH TO THE SOLU-
     TION OF PROBLEMS

A. Extent of thought about the problem
   1. Makes little or no use of hypotheses as to
      the correct solution.
   2. Makes little or no attempt to set up and
      use criteria which the solution must meet.
   3. Skips unfamiliar terms rather than make
      assumptions as to their possible meaning.
   4. Selects an answer on the basis of very
      few clues, or on the basis of superficial
      considerations.
   5. Selects an answer on the basis of "impres-
      sion" or "feelings" about what might be
      correct.
   6. Selects an answer because the other
      choices do not appear attractive.
   7. Selects an answer on the basis of random
      guesswork.
   8. Solves the problem without very much
      thought -- almost a mechanical solution.
   9. Gives little time to a consideration of the
      problem.
   10. Makes little or no attempt to reason about
       a problem because of lack of confidence
       in knowledge of the material.

(Frequency)
YES   NO   III. (Continued)   Comments

B. Care and system in thinking about the
   problem
   1. Makes little or no attempt to reorganize
      the problem in order to gain an under-
      standing of the material.
   2. Makes little or no attempt to delimit the
      possible answers or choices.
   3. Makes little attempt to break complex
      problems into more workable parts.
   4. Makes little attempt to deal with each
      part of a problem separately.
   5. Selects one of the choices offered and at-
      tempts to justify it.
   6. Starts the problem with no apparent plan
      for a solution.
   7. Jumps from one part of the problem to
      another part.
   8. Attacks the problem as a whole, reading
      directions, statement of the problem,
      and the alternatives again and again,
      searching for some clue to the solution.
   9. Neglects to consider important details in
      the solution.
   10. Careless in considering the details of the
       problem.
   11. Sidetracked by external considerations.
   12. Attempts to remember the solution to a
       similar problem rather than solving each
       problem independently.

C. Ability to follow through on a process of
   reasoning
   1. Carries reasoning part way through to
      completion, then gives up.
   2. Elaborates a hypothesis or the criteria
      for a solution but neglects to apply this
      reasoning to the selection of a final
      answer.
   3. Starts to solve the problem with a definite
      plan in mind, but loses sight of the orig-
      inal plan as difficulties are encountered.

IV. ATTITUDE TOWARD THE SOLUTION
    OF PROBLEMS

A. Attitude toward reasoning
   1. Takes the attitude that reasoning is of

(Frequency)			
YES	NO	IV. (Continued)	Comments

little value — one either knows the answer or does not.

2. Skips many problems, feeling that the
answers are purely a matter of information which is not possessed.

3. Believes it is unjustifiable to make certain assumptions to fill in gaps in information.

B. Confidence in ability to solve problems
1. Makes little attempt to attack the problems which appear to be complex and abstract.

2. Makes only a superficial attempt to reason through a problem, then gives up and
guesses.

3. Is unable to come to a definite conclusion
as to the answer or to decide between
two alternatives.

4. Has little confidence in the correctness
of the solution selected.

C. Introduction of personal considerations into
problem-solving
1. Has difficulty in maintaining an objective
attitude in certain problems because
personal opinions play an important part.

2. Has difficulty in differentiating between
correct answers and answers that seem
desirable on the basis of personal value
patterns.

3. Is distracted by many external considerations, such as opinion of the course, the
instructors, the examination, etc.